FEB 0 4 202 P9-CDL-274

NAPA COUNTY LIBRARY
580 COOMBS STREET
NAPA, CA 94559

ALSO BY JOHN LUTHER ADAMS

Winter Music: Composing the North

*The Place Where You Go to Listen: In Search of an
Ecology of Music*

SILENCES
SO DEEP

FARRAR, STRAUS AND GIROUX
New York

SILENCES

SO DEEP

MUSIC, SOLITUDE,
ALASKA

JOHN LUTHER ADAMS

Farrar, Straus and Giroux
120 Broadway, New York 10271

Copyright © 2020 by John Luther Adams
All rights reserved
Printed in the United States of America
First edition, 2020

Grateful acknowledgment is made for permission to reprint the
following material:
"Poem of the Forgotten" and portions of "Listening in October," by
John Haines, from *Winter News* (Middletown, CT: Wesleyan
University Press, 1966). Used by permission.
Lines from "In the Forest Without Leaves," by John Haines, from
The Owl in the Mask of the Dreamer: Collected Poems. Copyright © 1996
by John Haines. Reprinted with the permission of The Permissions
Company, LLC, on behalf of Graywolf Press, Minneapolis, Minnesota,
www.graywolfpress.org.

Photographs of the author with Cynthia Adams and the author with
Gordon Wright by Dennis Keeley. Photograph of the author with
John Haines by Charlie Backus.

Library of Congress Cataloging-in-Publication Data
Names: Adams, John Luther, 1953– author.
Title: Silences so deep : music, solitude, Alaska / John Luther Adams.
Description: First edition. | New York : Farrar, Straus and Giroux, [2020] |
    Includes bibliographical references.
Identifiers: LCCN 2020012294 | ISBN 9780374264628 (hardcover)
Subjects: LCSH: Adams, John Luther, 1953– | Composers—
    Alaska—Biography. | Alaska—Description and travel. | Wright,
    Gordon, 1934–2007. | Haines, John, 1924–2011. | LCGFT:
    Autobiographies.
Classification: LCC ML410.A2333 A3 2020 | DDC 780.92 [B]—dc23
LC record available at https://lccn.loc.gov/2020012294

Our books may be purchased in bulk for promotional, educational,
or business use. Please contact your local bookseller or the
Macmillan Corporate and Premium Sales Department at
1-800-221-7945, extension 5442, or by e-mail at
MacmillanSpecialMarkets@macmillan.com.

www.fsgbooks.com
www.twitter.com/fsgbooks • www.facebook.com/fsgbooks

10   9   8   7   6   5   4   3   2   1

For Cynthia, Gordon, and John

There are silences so deep

you can hear

the journeys of the soul,

enormous footsteps

downward in a freezing earth.

—JOHN HAINES

CONTENTS

Music in the Anthropocene

I am walking through a stunted spruce forest. On my back is a pack basket full of groceries. In each hand I carry a two-gallon jug of drinking water. Knee-high rubber boots keep my feet dry as I stride through the wet, spongy moss, but my broad-brimmed hat gives me precious little protection from the clouds of mosquitoes swirling around my head. Every hundred yards or so I stop, set the jugs down, and do a little tarantella to wave the bugs away. For a mile and a half I slog down the trail—along well-worn furrows, across a makeshift bridge over a small stream, up and down all the little dips and rises of the forest. At last I reach a short stretch of boardwalk. Soon I step onto the porch of a rough-cut cabin and set down my load. I am home.

I am twenty-eight years old. I've come here running away. Running away from my family. Running away from the cities and the suburbs. Running away from academia, and from the competitive world of "the music business." Coming here to this cabin in the boreal forest, I imagine that I'm running away from everything. But I'm actually running *to* everything. Here I will find the home I never had. I will also find my people, a ragtag and sometimes rowdy crew of musicians, poets, fishermen, and other kindred spirits we come to call the Ace Lake Sauna Society. And in time, I will come to discover the full shape of my life's work here.

———

Music is my way of understanding the world, of knowing where I
am and how I fit in. An unsettled childhood left me with a gnaw-
ing, inarticulate hunger to find my real home and family—the
place to which I would truly belong, and the people with whom I
would share ties deeper than blood. In Alaska—where I lived for
four decades—I found both.

In my twenties and into my thirties (in the 1970s and '80s),
I was a full-time environmental activist. The small role that I
played in the passage of the Alaska National Interest Lands Conservation Act (the largest land preservation law in history) and
in helping prevent destructive dams, highways, mining, and oil
drilling in Alaska remains among the most satisfying experiences
of my life.

But the time came when I realized that I had to choose between a life as an activist and a life as an artist. In that moment,
I decided that someone else could take my place in politics; and
no one else could make the music I imagined but me. So I took a
leap of faith, in the belief that music and art can matter every bit
as much as activism and politics.

An Inuit hunter scanning the tundra for game will tell you
that you learn the most by watching the edges. In Alaska I imagined I could work on the outer edge of culture, drawing my music more directly from the earth. I listened for that music in the
mountains and on the tundra, on the shoulders of glaciers and
the shores of the Arctic Ocean, and in the northern forest, learning the songs of the birds.

From the moment I arrived in Alaska, at the age of twenty-
two, I knew I would live there. And for much of my life, I
imagined I would die there. But the deaths of two dear friends,
changes in my own health, and a shrinking sense of possibility
in Alaskan society eventually compelled me to leave. At the turn
of the new century, as climate change began to accelerate, even

the extreme cold that made us feel special as Alaskans began to recede. Alaska was becoming too much like the country I had tried to escape.

Yet Alaska did not fail me. In spite of our broken frontier dreams, in spite of the destruction that we humans continue to visit on the land and the waters, the animals and the climate, Alaska is still Alaska. Any failure I may have felt in leaving Alaska was a failure of my own imagination.

And now I stand alone, on a beach far to the south, listening to the Pacific. As each wave rolls in—booming, roaring, growling, hissing—I listen to its voice: the unique contours of its rising and falling, its singular crescendo and diminuendo. I listen for the interval between this wave and the wave before it, and the one that comes after. I listen as the waves advance and retreat, melding and passing through one another, crashing like cymbals on the shore. I listen to the small stones clattering over one another, pulled inexorably back into the water that stretches away toward Asia.

I do my best to listen as intently, as deeply as I can. Even so, my mind wanders.

A plastic bottle among the rocks reminds me that there are vast islands of garbage drifting far out at sea. A strong gust of wind reminds me of the increasingly capricious weather, and of the storms that lash this and other shores with growing ferocity. The burning sunlight reminds me of melting tundra and expanding deserts, of diminishing polar ice and rising seas all over the earth.

How can I stand here today and not think of these things?

Yet, if you ask me if I'm composing a piece about climate change, I will tell you: "No. Not really."

Then is this music about the sea? Yes. Well, in a way . . . But what I really hope is that this music is an ocean of its own, an expansive sea of sound that just may carry the listener away into an oceanic state of mind.

As a composer, I believe that music has the power to inspire a renewal of human consciousness, culture, and politics. And yet I refuse to make political art. More often than not political art fails as politics, and all too often it fails as art. From the titles of my works—*songbirdsongs, In the White Silence, Become Ocean*— it's clear that I draw inspiration from the world around me. But when I enter my studio, I do so with the hope of leaving the world behind, at least for a while. Of course, it's impossible to sustain that state of grace for long. Inevitably, thoughts intrude: Sometimes I think about people, places, and experiences in my life—the independent souls and the frozen stillness, the solitude and camaraderie I knew in Alaska. Sometimes I think about the larger state of the world, and the uncertain future of humanity. And sometimes I think about the smaller world just outside my door.

If my music can draw people to be fully present, to listen deeply to this world that we share, then I will have done what I can as a composer to help us navigate this perilous era of our own creation.

For me, it all begins with listening.

| I |

Between Solitude and Politics

Early on the evening of April 4, 1968, while standing on the balcony of his motel room in Memphis, Tennessee, Martin Luther King, Jr., was assassinated. Two years later, on the anniversary of the assassination, my girlfriend and I climbed over the locked iron gate of our all-white boarding school on the north side of Atlanta and hitchhiked downtown to join the candlelight vigil at Ebenezer Baptist Church. She was a regular volunteer there in Dr. King's parish, and we were both frequent participants in civil rights and antiwar demonstrations around the city.

Dr. King was one of our great heroes. I knew that he had drawn inspiration from Mahatma Gandhi's practice of nonviolent resistance. I also knew that Gandhi had been inspired by Henry David Thoreau's essay "On the Duty of Civil Disobedience," which I'd first encountered in my ninth-grade literature class in New Jersey. I revisited that essay now with a deeper sense of purpose. And then I turned to *Walden*.

Thoreau's retreat to Walden, together with his outspoken opposition to slavery and the Mexican-American War, made it seem perfectly natural to me that an artist could work in solitude yet also be deeply engaged with the great social issues of his time. I still believe this, and throughout my life I've steered an uneasy course between the Scylla of solitude and the Charybdis of politics, between my desire to help change the world and my impulse to escape it. The vessel in which I navigate these turbulent waters is music.

Eventually, as the United States finally withdrew from the war in Vietnam, the passion that I'd felt marching in the streets of Atlanta would lead me to Alaska. I went north with big dreams—to be part of the campaign to save the last great wilderness in North America, and perhaps to help create a model for a new society. In Alaska, I also imagined that I could leave the world of contemporary culture behind, to search for a new kind of music drawn directly from the earth.

I grew up all over the eastern seaboard. My father had studied law and passed the bar exam, but he spent his professional life climbing the corporate ladder with the phone company (back in the days when there was only *one* phone company). For my younger brother and me, it was a bit like growing up in a military family. We moved around a lot.

I was born in Mississippi, but by the time I was three we were living in Atlanta. My first year of school found us in Columbia, South Carolina, where we rode out the Cuban Missile Crisis (with drills at school crouching under our desks), the Kennedy assassination, and the Beatles' first appearance on *The Ed Sullivan Show*. When I was in fourth grade, my dad was transferred to lower Manhattan, and the family moved into a small Tudor house in Short Hills, New Jersey. This was home for longer than any other place in my childhood.

In New Jersey I began to come of age. My friends and I lived in our own world, carving out identities in increasingly open rebellion against the values of our parents. (Years later, my mother said to me: "You divorced the family when you were fourteen.") We played in garage bands and listened to all kinds of edgy music. We read poetry and artsy literature. We experimented with drugs. And our aspirations turned us toward New York City, which beckoned like a shining mountain range on the horizon of our circumscribed suburban world.

We were regulars at the local record shop. Most afternoons we'd go there after school. LPs cost $1.79 apiece. We bought lots of them. The proprietor of the shop, Floyd, became our musical mentor. A real live old-school beatnik who sported a classic goatee and the occasional beret (as I recall, he was also openly gay), Floyd had musical knowledge and tastes that were up to the minute and wide-ranging. In his shop we discovered *Freak Out!*, the first album by Frank Zappa and the Mothers of Invention.

In the fine print on the jackets of those early Zappa albums, this defiant quote always appeared: "*The present-day composer refuses to die!*—Edgard Varèse."

We would scratch our heads and ask ourselves: "Just who *is* this Vah-REEZ-ee guy?"

Then we found the answer. Flipping through the bins in a Greenwich Village record shop, one of my pals came across an album with a photograph of a mad scientist on the cover. The man had long bushy brows rising above intense dark eyes, and a shock of thick wavy hair erupting from his forehead. The title on the disc was *The Music of Edgard Varèse   Volume Two.*

We soon tracked down *Volume One* as well. And we immersed ourselves in the fierce sonic geometries of *Intégrales*, *Ionisation*, and *Poème Électronique*. We devoured this music the same way we'd devour a new album by the Beatles. As soon as it would finish playing, we'd flip the record over and play it again. At first the sound was incomprehensible. There seemed to be no rhythm, no melody, no harmony, and no apparent logic to the way one sound followed another. I remember thinking: "There's nothing to grab on to here. I'll *never* be able to know where I am in this stuff!"

But after listening innumerable times we began to hear a few landmarks, certain distinctive constellations standing out amid the chaotic firmament: a single insistent tone from an oboe reiterated like Morse code, an irregular tattoo from a snare drum accented by unison outbursts from the other percussion, a jagged peak of brass and woodwinds piling up to a howling crescendo. We were learning how to listen and how to hear in the forbidding deserts of Varèse. From Varèse to Stravinsky, it didn't take us long to discover John Coltrane and John Cage, and a whole new world that twisted our ears and expanded our notions of just what music could be.

From the nearby station it was a short ride on the Erie-Lackawanna Railroad (with a transfer in Hoboken to the IRT "tube" train) to the wonders and temptations of Manhattan. (This was the same commute my father made every day to his office at the downtown headquarters of AT&T.) Whenever we could sneak away, my pals Richard Einhorn and Dennis Keeley and I made forbidden forays into the city. We were all rock drummers, so we'd occasionally go up to Forty-second Street to check out the instruments and buy drumheads, sticks, and hardware at Sam Ash or Manny's Music. Sometimes we'd go to hear the legendary street musician Moondog, who was usually in the neighborhood of Sixth Avenue and Fifty-third Street. But more often we'd make a beeline for the West Village.

We found out where Varèse had lived, in a narrow town house on Sullivan Street. We'd get off the subway at Christopher Street and walk directly to our hero's door. By this time, he was no longer alive. Still, we'd stand there, basking in his aura, waiting perhaps for the Sage of Sullivan Street to appear before us. To this day whenever I find myself in the West Village, I walk to 188 Sullivan. Next to the doorbell is a small engraved plate that reads: "Edgard Varèse lived here. 1925–1965." Standing at that door never fails to stir at least an echo of the awe that I felt as a kid.

The Village had been a mecca for the Beat Generation. And now it was a hothouse for the nascent hippies. The folk scene was thriving in clubs like the Bottom Line. The greats of jazz were playing at the Village Vanguard. The Mothers and the Fugs would occasionally appear at various joints in the neighborhood. Now and then my underage buddies and I managed to finagle our way into places we had no business being. But mostly we just walked around, our mouths agape, among the ragged longhairs, exotic/erotic-looking women, flamboyant cross-dressers, street-corner preachers, and socialist orators. Just passing through Washington Square was titillating, exhilarating, and a little bit intimidating. My pals and I always picked up *The Village Voice* or, better yet, *The East Village Other*. It made us feel like we really belonged there. We bought records. We bought drugs on street corners. We got our money taken by con men. Yet somehow we never got ourselves into serious trouble.

And then one evening in 1968 my dad came home and announced that the company had transferred him to Macon, Georgia. I felt as though the world as I knew it was coming to an end.

Both my parents were alcoholics. In Georgia, their drinking escalated. So did my rebellion. And as my parents' marriage began to come apart, I got booted out of two prep schools—first in Macon, then in Atlanta: the one where my girlfriend and I scaled the wall to join that candlelight vigil in memory of Dr. King. I never graduated from high school but somehow, at eighteen, I found myself in the music school at the newly established California Institute of the Arts.

As I started at CalArts, my girlfriend, Margrit, entered UCLA as an engineering student. We'd found ourselves an apartment on West Palm Avenue in West Hollywood, just a block downhill from the Sunset Strip. Our parents pretended not to know we were living together in the fleshpots of decadence. We pretended to be adults.

Each day I made the commute, by L.A. city bus and Greyhound, from Hollywood up to CalArts, fifty miles north. The Sylmar earthquake of 1971 had killed sixty-five people in the San Fernando Valley, and laid waste to a dam, two hospitals, and two freeway interchanges, which still lay as huge piles of rubble along my daily route. At the Greyhound station I'd listen for the announcement of my bus, sung out by a stentorian baritone, like something right out of a piece by Harry Partch: *"San Fernando, Newhall, Saugus, Palmdale, Lancaster, Mojave, Inyokern, Lone Pine, Independence, Big Pine, Bishop . . ."*

I loved the poetry of those names and the places they conjured in my imagination—sere, empty desert places; clean, high mountain places that I longed to see, places in the much larger world out there beyond the teeming Los Angeles basin. I dreamed of staying on the bus past my stop and disappearing into those open spaces. But that would have to wait. Right now, for the first time ever, all I did was music.

Before CalArts I'd unconsciously subscribed to the notion that to be truly new and interesting music had to be complicated. Now here I was surrounded by music that was formally simple yet sonically rich and bracingly new. In my teacher James Tenney's *Having Never Written a Note for Percussion*, for instance, a single protracted swell on a tam-tam revealed a rainbow of sonic colors. The music of the faculty members Harold Budd and Charlemagne Palestine, as well as that of my classmates Peter Garland and Michael Byron, was similarly exciting. The fact that this music was both intelligent and immediately alluring helped me understand what until then had been more of a concept than a real conviction: Music is all about sound.

I entered a piece in a contest sponsored by the San Jose chapter of the American Guild of Organists. Several months later I received a letter informing me that I'd won second prize. I was thrilled. There was a cash award of $250, and the piece would be performed and recorded. Most exciting, the primary judge had been none other than Lou Harrison, who by this time had become one of my musical heroes. I wasn't wild about my organ piece, but the fact that Lou Harrison had apparently liked it was a tremendous encouragement to me. Emboldened, I made the pilgrimage to San Jose, where Lou was teaching at the time. I was delighted to find the man himself every bit as scintillating and engaging as his music. His matter-of-fact embrace of my aspirations removed any shred of doubt that I would make a life as a composer.

If the pinewoods of Georgia had felt like a cultural desert to me, the arid landscapes of Southern California felt like a lush forest. I'd never been exposed to so much music and so many musicians in one place. But I was there for just two years. My father had never bought the idea that his rock drummer son could make a life as a composer. He'd always hoped I'd become a lawyer. So, facing a contentious divorce and a large settlement, my dad decided he no longer wanted to subsidize me at one of the most expensive and "experimental" schools in the country. I didn't argue. It wouldn't have done me any good. Besides, I was ready to escape the buzzing sprawl of Los Angeles. I applied for accelerated graduation, and in the spring of 1973, at the age of twenty, I was among the first class of students to graduate from CalArts. Then I got out of L.A. as quickly as I could.

While I was there, the California condor was teetering on the verge of extinction (as a result of habitat loss and DDT contamination). Some years later a captive breeding program would manage to restore a small population of the great birds, which

now seem to be holding their own. But at that time the last few
individuals in the wild lived in Los Padres National Forest, not far
from CalArts. I became obsessed with the condors. Although I
never saw one, they came to represent to me the fate of the original place that was so rapidly disappearing beneath the rapacious
expansion of Los Angeles.

The whole time I was there, I had a hollow feeling in the pit of
my stomach. I blamed this on L.A. Eventually, though, I would
come to understand that the hollowness wasn't really in the place.
It was in me.

Soon enough, I found myself back in Georgia, living with
my girlfriend in an old farmhouse in the countryside south of
Atlanta. A few hours a week I worked at the public library in the
nearby town of Stockbridge. (I was *the* librarian. If I wasn't there,
the library wasn't open.) But I spent most of my days working
as a farmhand for our landlord, the old mule trader J. Waymon
Stokes, and tending a half-acre garden of organic vegetables that
I worked with a donkey named Jerry—selling what Margrit and I
couldn't use to specialty markets and restaurants.

Early each morning and again around sunset, I would walk,
among oaks and poplars, sycamores and flowering dogwoods. At
the edge of the woods and out in the fields were choruses of birds.
But most often I would walk farther into the trees, following sil-
very, limpid phrases that floated through the cool air. Now and
then I would catch a glimpse of the singer, always deeper in the
forest. This music filled me with longing, an aching hunger to
feel at home in the world. In time I learned that this was the
wood thrush—the favorite singer of my hero Thoreau. I listened
to this music for weeks before trying to write down something of
what I was hearing and feeling.

In time, with the aid of a field guide and binoculars, I learned which birds sang which songs. I began to recognize the distinctive voices of the cardinal, Carolina wren, eastern towhee, tufted titmouse, redwing blackbird, and eastern meadowlark. Following my studies at CalArts, my teachers now were the birds. With the self-consciousness of the young artist, I assiduously avoided the music of Olivier Messiaen and other composers who had incorporated birdsong into their music. I chose not to use field recordings to help with my notations. I began to carry a music notebook on my walks. I wanted to take dictation directly from the birds themselves—as Annie Dillard writes: "learning the strange syllables one by one."

Margrit was the younger daughter of Wernher von Braun, who was then directing the U.S. government space program in Huntsville, Alabama. (When I'd fallen for her at that boarding school in Atlanta, I'd never even heard of her father.) Margrit and I had been living together for several years when, in spite of her father's disapproval, we decided to get married. The ceremony took place at the justice of the peace in Folkston, Georgia—the gateway to Okefenokee Swamp. Our honeymoon was a canoe trip across the swamp. Soon, my pal Ernie Collins and I began making regular trips into Okefenokee, and floating rivers throughout southern Georgia—the Satilla, the St. Mary's, the Suwanee, and the Flint. We made backpacking trips in the Appalachians of north Georgia, and in the Tetons of Wyoming. Then, in the summer of 1975, we made the trip that changed my life.

Ever since encountering the film version of Glenn Gould's *The Idea of North*, I'd dreamed of traveling in northern Canada and Alaska. Now, in *Audubon* magazine and *The Sierra Club Bulletin*, I was reading more and more about the campaign to preserve large areas of wilderness in Alaska. My imagination was captivated, and I wanted to experience Alaska for myself.

In early July, Ernie and I flew north. As the plane touched down in Juneau, I caught my first glimpse of the Mendenhall Glacier, tumbling off the ice field. Within an hour we were hiking up its west ridge. The spruce-scented air was intoxicating, and I was astonished by the deep cobalt blue of the ice. As we climbed amid boulders, rubble, and orange columbine, my ear caught a faint tinkling—like glass wind chimes in a gentle breeze. Looking down, I realized it was meltwater, resonating from deep within a crevasse. Such a delicate sound for such an immensity of ice! In that moment of epiphany, I knew that something fundamental had changed.

For the next week we paddled and portaged our way across Admiralty Island, through a chain of jewel-like lakes. The old-growth rain forest of spruce, fir, and hemlock was filled with a luxuriant stillness, occasionally punctuated by the excited percolations of winter wrens, the cascading arpeggios of hermit thrushes, and the low drumming of ruffed grouse. As I traveled on through Alaska—to Denali, Glacier Bay, and Katmai—I imagined there was music that could be heard only there, music that belonged there like the plants and the birds, music that resonated with all that space and silence, cold and stone, wind and fire and ice. I longed to hear that music, to follow it wherever it might lead me.

Back in Georgia, I began composing a piece for organ and two percussionists that would eventually become my first orchestral work. I also became active in environmental politics. The U.S. Army Corps of Engineers had proposed building a major dam at Sprewell Bluff on the Flint River. I knew the river well from my canoe trips with Ernie. And it wasn't long before I found myself lobbying against the dam in the Georgia legislature, and sitting in on a meeting with Governor Jimmy Carter. The governor was outspoken in his opposition to the Sprewell Bluff dam, and, ultimately, we succeeded in stopping the project. I was so impressed with Mr. Carter that when he later announced his intention to run for president, I volunteered for his campaign—going door-to-door in the swing states of Arkansas, Oklahoma, and New Mexico. I also became active as a volunteer with the Alaska Coalition, giving presentations to local groups, encouraging people to write to Congress in support of the pending legislation.

Although I was determined to live in Alaska, my wife wasn't so sure about that idea. She applied for jobs throughout the west, and in 1976 she accepted a position with the State of Idaho Department of Environmental Quality. It wasn't Alaska. Still, it was a step in the right direction. I went to work as a ranch hand for our new landlord, Herb MacDowell. And I spent most of the following summer where I really wanted to be.

To prepare me for grassroots rabble-rousing and for lobbying in Congress, the Wilderness Society invited me along as "conservation director" on two excursions in Alaska. My first trip that summer was in the Arctic National Wildlife Range (now the Arctic National Wildlife Refuge). The trip leader was Ginny Hill Wood. Ginny and her partner Celia Hunter had first come north as pilots, flying military cargo planes to Fairbanks just after World War II. When the temperature dropped to minus 60 degrees Fahrenheit, there were no flights back to Seattle. So they decided to stay in Alaska. Together with Ginny's husband, Woody Wood, they established Camp Denali, a wilderness lodge in what is now Denali National Park.

In the late 1950s the federal government had proposed two nightmare projects in Alaska: the massive Rampart Dam on the Yukon River, and Project Chariot—using nuclear warheads to blast a deepwater port near Nome. In response, Ginny and Woody hosted a meeting in their living room that led to the founding of the Alaska Conservation Society (ACS), the first such group in the state. In 1960, Ginny (together with Margaret Murie, Justice William O. Douglas, and others) convinced President Eisenhower to take executive action to establish the Arctic National Wildlife Range. Ginny was a legend in Alaska conservation. She must've wondered about this eager young buck who'd been assigned as her assistant. But it didn't take long for Ginny and Celia to become mother figures for me, as they were for so many of us younger Alaskans.

During that second summer in Alaska, I also met Gordon Wright. Gordon had come north in 1969, to teach at the University of Alaska Fairbanks, and to serve as music director of the Fairbanks Symphony Orchestra. Before long, he had created the Arctic Chamber Orchestra—a smaller ensemble designed to foster cultural exchange in village Alaska. And in 1971, amid the frenzy over construction of the Trans-Alaska Pipeline, Gordon and others had established the Fairbanks Environmental Center.

Over lunch, Gordon endorsed my determination to live in Alaska and encouraged me to settle in Fairbanks. He told me all about his life in his cabin in the woods a few miles west of town. Although we environmentalists were decisively outnumbered here, Gordon told me that I would find a strong community of like-minded people who were working hard to make a difference in the future of the young state. Over the next year, when I was back on the ranch in Idaho, Gordon and I exchanged letters. He told me more about life in Fairbanks and encouraged me to keep looking for a way to make my home there.

The following spring Margrit told me that she needed a "timeout" from our marriage. Not long after that, I received a letter from Gordon, who told me that the Fairbanks Environmental Center was looking for a new executive director, and that he and others were convinced that I was the guy for the job. I headed north.

All I knew was that someone from the Environmental Center would meet me at the airport. That someone turned out to be Cindy Marquette. I had met Cindy in Idaho, where she and I led a couple of Alaska Coalition workshops together. We'd been out of touch for a while, and I had no idea that Cindy was back in Alaska. But here she was, working at the Environmental Center, as irrepressible and alluring as ever.

We began with small talk about my flight and the weather. Then Cindy asked me about my wife.

I heaved an existential sigh: "It looks like we're breaking up."

"I'm sorry . . ." she replied.

There was an awkward silence.

Dutifully, I inquired about her husband. It was Cindy's turn to look sad.

"Oh. We broke up."

There was a longer, heavier pause.

The Environmental Center had been founded in response to the construction of the Trans-Alaska Pipeline. But now that the oil was flowing, the young organization was grappling with a dizzying array of issues—from destructive mining in pristine watersheds and proposed highways into wild country, to the aerial hunting of wolves and the reckless sales of public land by the State of Alaska. I was already the favorite son of the Center's founding fathers, Jim Kowalsky and Gordon Wright. My formal interview and informal meetings with board members went well. But there were other candidates for the job, and the board was determined to exercise their due diligence. I'd planned to do the interview in Fairbanks and then continue on out to Nome, to spend the winter with my pal Ernie Collins. But Cindy had been working at the Center for quite a while without much help. So I volunteered to stay for a month and pitch in.

There was no rush for me to get to Nome. Besides, I figured this would be a kind of working audition. It would give the folks at the Center a longer look at me. And it would give me a taste of Fairbanks in the winter. The board insisted on paying me, and Ginny and Celia welcomed me into the guest cabin at Dogpatch—their little homestead in the woods north of town. It felt great to be in Alaska again. I threw myself into the work, and I finally left for Nome just before the winter solstice.

In those days, there were no direct flights from Fairbanks to Nome. Wien Air Alaska flew from Anchorage to Kotzebue, and then back down to Nome. For some reason, we deplaned in Kotzebue. There was no Jetway. The tiny terminal building was about a hundred yards from the back door of the plane. The temperature was minus 45, and the wind was blowing 45 miles an hour—making the wind chill factor about 90 degrees below zero. The runway was solid ice, and the wind was blowing a whiteout of hard snow directly into our faces. It was the Arctic version of one of those Sahara windstorm scenes in the movies, where the camels disappear into the blinding sand. I was wearing a heavy parka with the big ruffed hood pulled tight. Even so, about halfway to the terminal, I remember thinking: "I may not make it." By the time I stumbled through the doorway, I had the worst ice-cream headache of my life. It felt as if my eyeballs had frozen solid in their sockets.

My old canoeing buddy Ernie welcomed me to Nome as though he'd been waiting for a while—which, in a way, he had. On our first trip north three years earlier, both Ernie and I had decided that Alaska was the place for us. By the end of that year he had moved north. Now he was working as a counselor for the state Department of Health and Social Services, living in a plain but warm little house not far from the famous Front Street finish line of the Iditarod sled dog race. My tiny bedroom doubled as my studio, where I worked on *A Northern Suite*—the orchestral piece I'd begun sketching that first summer in Alaska.

Nome sits right on the shore of Norton Sound, in the northern Bering Sea, and it's regularly hammered by strong weather. After one especially heavy storm, Ernie and I spent several hours digging a tunnel to rescue a woman whose house on Front Street was completely buried under hard-crusted snow.

The winter nights were long, and there wasn't much to do in Nome. So after dinner we usually walked over to Ernie's favorite bar, the Board of Trade—also known as the "B-O-T" or, alternately, the "Bottom of the Toilet." It was a genial-enough dive, and surprisingly low-key for such a rough-and-tumble town. Even so, playing pool, drinking beer, and listening to bar bands went only so far.

Cabin fever was a very real problem, and I made a special point to get outside and soak up whatever sunlight I could. Each day I would go out for a spin on my cross-country skis. The snow in the woods around Fairbanks had been a lovely light powder. Out here on the shore of the Bering Sea, it was a heavy blanket encrusted in a thick, glassy shell of ice. And it seemed like the wind was always blowing. I remember one gusty afternoon standing erect, skiing uphill *backward*, without moving a muscle.

One day I skied out onto frozen Norton Sound, where I met a Yup'ik elder who was ice fishing for tanner crabs. There was no shelter. But I stood there for hours, talking with the old man, occasionally removing the slush to keep the hole from freezing over, helping him pull up the pots full of crabs—getting a glimpse into an older way of life.

These were still the days of the Cold War between the United States and the Soviet Union. But in the villages of Gambell and Savoonga on St. Lawrence Island, people had relatives in the Chukotka region of Siberia—less than forty miles across the Bering Strait. At the islands of Big Diomede and Little Diomede, the distance between the USA and the USSR was less than three miles. I loved that the local radio station, KNOM, made announcements in three different languages—English, Yup'ik, and Siberian Yup'ik. We were definitely *not* in Kansas.

Although Nome is hardly a garden spot, in my unmitigated romanticism its funkiness seemed charming. But Ernie was more directly in touch with the darker side of life out here. His professional circuit included Elim, Shaktoolik, Unalakleet, Stebbins, and other villages in the region, and the problems he encountered were heartbreaking. Alcoholism, drug abuse, and domestic violence were widespread in these communities torn between their traditional lifeways, of subsistence hunting and fishing, and the recent arrival of television and consumer commodities. Even so, when Ernie invited me to fly with him down the coast to the village of Golovin, I leaped at the opportunity.

We boarded a Cessna 185, the ubiquitous single-engine workhorse of "bush" Alaska. Ernie and I were the only passengers. As we took off, our pilot said the weather might be "touch and go." Within minutes, it was far more touch than go. A squall moved in. Snow started swirling. We slipped through a couple of holes in the clouds. But the ceiling continued to descend, and so did we. Our pilot fell silent. And I had to remind myself to keep breathing. We turned back toward Nome, looking for any discernible sign of the earth below us. And ten or fifteen tense minutes later we touched back down on the runway, just as the visibility fell to zero.

A few years later Ernie's future wife, Mary Pat, would find herself in similar conditions on a flight between the villages of Ambler and Shungnak. She was the only survivor. Flights like these are an all-too-familiar fact of life in rural Alaska.

In mid-February, Ernie and I decided to make an overnight ski trip on the tundra. The weather was cold but clear. The snow was perfect for building an igloo, and we managed to fashion a shelter in which we passed a relatively comfortable night. In the wee hours I woke to hear Ernie somewhere outside the igloo, whooping like a madman. When he shouted, "Adams! Get out here right now!" my first thought was: "Oh no. A polar bear!"

I bolted from the igloo. In the sky directly overhead, brilliant rays of phosphorescent red, purple, yellow, and green were shooting out in all directions. The movement accelerated and the colors grew more intense. Then everything started to spin.

Later that winter, I received a letter offering me the position of executive director of the Fairbanks Environmental Center. I flew back to Idaho. Although Margrit wasn't ready to call it quits for good, she wasn't yet ready to move forward with our marriage, either. So in March 1979 I pointed my pickup truck north. The heartbreak was still fresh, but mixed with my tears was a growing sense of excitement. Driving the Alaska Highway in winter felt like a grand adventure. I was finally making the move I'd dreamed about for years.

Following the first Earth Day, the early 1970s was a time of landmark environmental legislation in the United States. The National Environmental Policy Act, the Endangered Species Act, the Clean Water Act, and an expanded Clean Air Act all passed Congress in relatively rapid succession. Alaska's Native peoples had struggled for years to gain recognition of their indigenous rights. Finally, when oil was discovered at Prudhoe Bay, those rights began to be addressed, and in 1971 Congress passed the Alaska Native Claims Settlement Act.

The Native Claims Act also authorized the secretary of the interior to withdraw large tracts of public land for environmental protection. This gave birth to an unprecedented grassroots campaign to preserve complete wild ecosystems in Alaska. The Alaska Coalition was a nationwide alliance of scientific, labor, and environmental organizations, as well as Alaska Native groups dedicated to protecting their home ground and traditional cultures. As an activist with the Coalition, I gave interviews on television and radio and to newspapers. I wrote articles and pamphlets. I organized and spoke at community workshops throughout the country. I lobbied in Congress.

Many elected officials stepped forward to provide leadership for the Alaska wild lands legislation—most notably Congressman Morris Udall and President Carter. Just before Ronald Reagan took office as president, the leadership pushed a compromise version of the legislation through Congress. And on December 8, 1980, President Carter signed the Alaska National Interest Lands Conservation Act (ANILCA) into law. It wasn't perfect. There were some serious omissions, most notably the lack of Wilderness protection for the coastal plain of the Arctic National Wildlife Refuge, leaving this priceless landscape open for oil and gas exploration. Even so, ANILCA was the single largest land preservation act in history, setting aside 104 million acres of original Alaska. With one stroke of the pen it more than doubled the size of the National Park system. This would be impossible in today's political environment, no matter which party might control the Congress or who might be in the White House.

When I first arrived, in the summer of 1975, Alaska had been a state for just sixteen years. It had the youngest and fewest people of any state. The mean age of Alaskans was twenty-eight, and the population was about 376,000—a little more than half of what it is today. Alaska was the richest state, and the most educated of the United States. Despite its outsized geography, the whole of Alaska felt like a single small town. Wherever you might travel in the state, you were always around people you knew. And even though you might have diametrically opposite worldviews, if someone was pulled over by the side of the road, people would always stop to offer help.

The elegantly conceived Alaska Constitution had set a broad-minded tone of open government. Traditional party lines didn't mean much. The governor, Jay Hammond, was a committed conservationist. Although he was nominally Republican, Hammond's views on the role of government inclined toward a kind of democratic socialism. Representation in the state legislature encompassed a wide range of views, and ordinary citizens had direct access to their elected officials. The Trans-Alaska Pipeline was not yet under construction. The *Exxon Valdez* was only a doomsday scenario. The multi-year ice pack on the Arctic Ocean had not yet begun to recede. And global warming was still a theoretical possibility, discussed only in the most rarefied scientific circles.

Now, with the money from the Trans-Alaska Pipeline in full flow, the State of Alaska was filthy rich. And many Alaska politicians had big plans for that money. Our mission at the Environmental Center was to try to prevent them from realizing the worst of those plans. My primary collaborator in this crusade was the spirited woman who would eventually become my wife.

It didn't take long for Cindy and me to stake out a new and much broader geographic territory for our organization. We persuaded the board of directors to change the name from the Fairbanks Environmental Center to the Northern Alaska Environmental Center. We changed our mission statement to encompass all of the state from the crest of the Alaska Range north to the Arctic Ocean—an area more than one and a half times the size of Texas. Proclaiming ourselves "the environmental voice of northern Alaska," we drew our motto from a poem by Gary Snyder: *Behind is a forest that goes to the Arctic . . . / And here we must draw / Our line.* With these words we struck a more radical posture on the issues, distinguishing ourselves from the older, increasingly conservative Alaska Conservation Society.

The names alone told the story. "Conservation" dated from the Teddy Roosevelt era, the old school that advocated "wise management of our natural resources." But we were "environmentalists," a new generation of activists committed to preserving complete ecosystems and to creating a sustainable, post-petroleum society in Alaska. We drew a lot of criticism. We also drew more members, and more active volunteers. Celia and Ginny, the founding mothers of ACS, told us to take the lead and run, and gave us their full support. Ginny began writing a regular column for our newsletter. Before long, the ACS folded.

One by one, biologists, geologists, and other scientists who worked in government agencies or at the University of Alaska began coming surreptitiously into our offices to express their deepest concerns. We became their public voice.

Cindy kept the organization running. And I was the front man.

Once, I and a couple of my male colleagues from the Environmental Center went to a meeting with executives of a major oil company who had flown in from headquarters to try to reach a compromise with us on something or other. We greenies arrived in our nicest, freshly pressed suits. And as the oilmen walked in decked out in shiny jeans, clean hiking boots, and brand-new flannel shirts, I remembered Thoreau's admonition: "Beware of all enterprises that require new clothes."

The office that we rented upstairs from an insurance broker was a disaster. The rust-orange water that flowed from the tap was undrinkable. The toilet didn't work. And the cheap construction was falling down around us. Eventually we took our landlord to small claims court. We won, and improvements were forthcoming. But we decided it was time to stop paying rent and buy a place of our own. Cindy solicited contributions from board members and other supporters, and we paid $30,000 cash for a small house at 218 Driveway Street—on the wrong side of the Alaska Railroad tracks—in the shadow of the *Fairbanks Daily News-Miner* building. We were pleased to be a thorn in their side.

In those days we were regular targets on the editorial page of the *Snooze-Minus* (as we called it). In April 1980, when the Environmental Center sponsored a local celebration of the tenth anniversary of Earth Day, the newspaper ran an editorial calling us "Communist sympathizers." (This was especially amusing, since the Boy Scouts of America was among the groups joining the celebration.) In another editorial I was personally singled out as "a carpetbagger with no roots in the community."

Cindy had studied journalism and worked for newspapers in Colorado and Idaho. Our monthly newsletter, *The Northern Line*, was her pride and joy. It became so notable that it received several awards from the Alaska Press Club, which must have caused a little bit of a buzz in the editorial room across the street.

In the 1970s I was a regular reader of the weekly newspaper the *Alaska Advocate*. Published by a small band of young firebrands (including my friend, the future editor of the *Anchorage Daily News*, Howard Weaver), the *Advocate* offered an essential alternative to the industrial-development propaganda that appeared in the grim pages of the *Anchorage Daily Times* and the *Fairbanks*

Daily News-Miner. The *Advocate* also provided encouraging evidence that there was intelligent life in Alaska, people who thought about things beyond the next big pipeline or mining boom.

Working on a frayed shoestring budget, the *Advocate* made valiant efforts to investigate and expose the bad public policies, corruption, and collusion between government and business that were so rampant in Alaska. Beyond the feature stories and editorials, I enjoyed the sardonic humor writing and the insightful musical musings in "Contrapunctus"—the regular column by my friend the conductor Gordon Wright.

It was in the *Advocate*, sometime in 1977, that I'd come across a review of *Cicada*—a new book by the poet John Haines. I hadn't read Haines before, but I was so taken by the excerpts in the review that I immediately tracked down a copy. At the time I was still living in Idaho, on a ranch on the Nez Perce Reservation. I remember walking the hills reading aloud, reveling in the deep resonances of Haines's words and the images they evoked. I soon acquired two of his earlier books, *The Stone Harp* and *Winter News*. The latter especially haunted me, with its visions of the north as a place to rediscover our ancient roots in the earth and imagine new possibilities for the human spirit.

All that summer, on my travels throughout the Arctic Wildlife Range and in the Gates of the Arctic, I had carried *Winter News* in my backpack. I read those poems over and over again, until I came to feel that they belonged to me. Now I read them out loud to my new love, Cindy, on our first camping trip together in the Alaska Range, not far from the homestead where the poet had lived for some twenty-five years. Haines had left the homestead in 1969, so during my first years in Alaska, he was a specter, an oracle speaking truth about place and imagination, challenging and inspiring me to a deeper sense of possibility in my own life's work. One of my favorite poems in *Winter News* was "Listening in October." The final stanza was especially evocative for me.

> There are silences so deep
> you can hear
> the journeys of the soul,
> enormous footsteps
> downward in a freezing earth.

I longed to hear more of those silences, to experience some of those journeys, and somehow to evoke them in music.

At the Environmental Center, we printed these words in a fundraising mailer. The response to that appeal was strong. But the real prize came one morning in the spring of 1980 when John Haines himself walked through the door of our office in the rickety little house at 218 Driveway. After a decade wandering in the wilderness of the outside world—living in California and Montana, and traveling here and there—Alaska's poet had come home.

At that first meeting, John gave us a lovely little essay titled "Ice," which we published in *The Northern Line*. John and I sat for a long while in the backyard, getting acquainted, talking about music and writing, and resolving to get together again, soon. For a short while, John stayed at the cabin of our friend Henry Cole, out at Nine-Mile Chena Hot Springs Road. But John had returned to Alaska with the dream of resuming his previous life at the homestead. And before long he had managed to rent the place from the woman to whom he had sold it a decade before. There we began a friendship that lasted some thirty-two years.

The Environmental Center had helped citizens in the fishing town of Homer in their successful campaign to stop oil and gas leasing in Kachemak Bay. So to return the favor, a group of fishermen from Homer drove a truckload of shrimp and crab up to

Fairbanks for a fundraising event. Our Shrimp and Crab Feed was held at the Pump House Restaurant. The weather was good and the turnout was great. Several hundred people showed up for the fresh, all-you-can-eat seafood, and to support the good cause.

The kitchen of the Pump House was buzzing, filled with the Center's staff and volunteers working madly to try to keep up with the demand from the crowd. The phone rang. One of us answered it. The voice on the other end said: "There's a bomb in the Pump House. And it's gonna blow all you goddamn environmentalists to kingdom come!" (*Click.*)

We had no choice but to take this seriously. We called the police. They told us to evacuate the restaurant and wait for the officers to arrive. We did.

When the officers arrived, our crowd was still standing on the lawn on the riverbank, happily munching away. After discussing the situation for a few minutes, the cops told us that the only way we could bring people back into the restaurant to continue the event was to conduct a thorough search of the premises. That sounded reasonable to us. Then they told us that they would stay outside with the crowd. And that *we* were the ones who would go back inside and conduct the search!

Recognizing that we didn't have much choice, that's exactly what we did. We turned that restaurant upside down. We looked in all the cabinets. We looked in all the ovens. We looked in the refrigerators. We looked under the bar. We looked in all the trash cans. Eventually, we came to the conclusion that there probably was no bomb. So the people came back in. The cops left. And the feast continued, without further incident. Today it's unthinkable that police anywhere in the United States could behave that way without repercussions. But this was Pipeline-era Alaska, and we environmentalists were viewed by many of our neighbors as personae non gratae.

Even so, in those days it wasn't difficult for committed young people to actually make a difference in politics in Alaska. I was appointed to advisory committees for state and federal agencies. We had regular meetings with the governor and members of the legislature. I was even involved in drafting bills that actually became law. It was a heady experience. But no one told us that we couldn't do these things. We just did them.

The state coffers were overflowing, and the legislature was a free-for-all of proposed industrial development projects. The Reagan administration was also doing its best to open unprotected lands and waters to oil drilling, mining, and logging. We were surprisingly successful at stopping them. We helped keep oil and gas drilling out of fish-rich Bristol Bay and the ice-laden Chukchi Sea. We prevented the Trans-Alaska Pipeline Haul Road from becoming an open corridor for motorized vehicles and sport hunting. We helped prevent state land sales (so-called land disposals) that would've destroyed important wildlife habitat. Perhaps most incredibly, we prevented the Alaska Power Authority from building what would have been the two largest dams in the world, back-to-back, on the Susitna River.

Between full-time crusading and cabin living, there was little time for anything else in those days, including music. But I remember one magical afternoon in May 1979, sitting in the birch-and-aspen forest outside our cabin, listening to the singing of a hermit thrush. I knew this song from my travels in the cloud forest of Southeast Alaska, eight hundred miles to the south. But here in these younger, leaner woods, the phrases were longer and more florid, and the tones were brighter—like the light flickering through the newly opened leaves. This singer was clearly related to the wood thrush—the bird that had started it all for me in Georgia. Now, here in my new home, this music seemed to touch me even more deeply. And in the years since then, I've often said that the music I want to hear when I finally depart this world is the song of the hermit thrush. For me, this is the music of heaven.

I sat listening for a long time. Then I opened my notebook and began writing down the bird's music as I heard it, with piccolos and violins in mind. The gentle swaying of the trees struck me as slower echoes of the thrush, and I sketched them for soft chimes. The long, sustained whistles of a varied thrush, I scored for crotales (antique cymbals) to be played with a contrabass bow. Deeper in the woods, a ruffed grouse began drumming. I scored this for a log drum. Before long, I had *Evensong*, my first piece composed entirely in Alaska and the final piece in the collection *songbirdsongs*. The following year (1980), an ensemble of friends and I recorded all of those pieces for release as an LP—my first published recording.

To stay in touch with what we were working to protect, Cindy and I traveled out into wild Alaska whenever we could. In the summer of 1980, we set out with my friend the photographer Wilbur Mills and his then-wife, Molly McCammon, from the headwaters of the Kobuk River—Walker Lake, near the Gates of the Arctic. Molly and Wilbur were in an aluminum canoe with a small motor. Cindy and I paddled a heavy double kayak. The plan was to float a couple of hundred miles to the village of Ambler, where we'd pick up another canoe and motor, then continue up the Ambler River to Molly and Wilbur's cabin near the crest of the Brooks Range. Until we reached Ambler there was no way Cindy and I could keep pace with the canoe. So we all kicked back and enjoyed a leisurely trip down the Upper Kobuk. But by the time we approached the Nunamiut village of Kobuk, Wilbur was ready to fire up the motor and rev on down to Ambler.

A mile or two above Kobuk we made camp. Even today Kobuk is one of the more remote villages in Alaska. Back then outside visitors were just beginning to appear. Understandably, local residents were not sure what to make of this, and cross-cultural tensions could sometimes be high. (Earlier that summer a couple camping near Barrow had been murdered in their tent.) During the night we were startled awake by gunshots and angry voices shouting from a boat idling in the river. All we could do was to hug the ground and stay quiet. After what seemed an eternity, the shooting and shouting stopped and the boat motored away.

The next morning Wilbur and Molly zipped on into Kobuk. Cindy and I brought up the rear in our heavy freighter. When we finally arrived, we beached the boat and walked into the village. We were passing by a small cabin when a flaming Coleman stove came flying out an open window and landed on the path right in front of us. The stove was followed by a string of flaming epithets and a diminutive Iñupiaq man who appeared on the porch in hot pursuit. When he saw a tall bearded stranger standing there in a broad-brimmed hat, he stopped, looked me up and down, and snarled: "I don't give a fuck who you are! I don't give a fuck if you're BLM, or *who* the fuck you are!"

I apologized for any intrusion and explained that we weren't with the government. Then we quickly continued on our way, followed by a relentless stream of invective.

Unsettled by this incident and the events of the night before, Cindy and I were eager to get back on the river. We returned to the boats. After a while Wilbur appeared and announced that he'd arranged a "ride" for us to Ambler. An hour or so later who should appear? None other than the man with the flaming stove, accompanied by a larger buddy.

I took Wilbur aside and expressed my reservations, but he laughed me off. As he and Molly hopped in their canoe and roared away, they waved and called out: "See you in Ambler!"

Cindy and I looked at each other, wondering if they'd *ever* see us again.

Although I'd removed my hat and packed it into the kayak,

there was no question that Flaming Stove Man and I recognized each other. Still, nothing was said about earlier events. We introduced ourselves. He was Thomas Mouse. His friend was Don Sheldon.

Cindy and I lifted our kayak into their large flat-bottomed riverboat and we were on our way. In a matter of minutes Don and Thomas produced a full bottle of Ronrico rum and began sipping. They asked if Cindy and I wanted a sip. She declined.

To her surprise, I said, "Sure." I wasn't much of a drinker, but I reasoned that the more I drank, the less there would be for our river pilots to drink. Meanwhile, Cindy's thinking was: "Oh great. Now I'll have *three* drunk guys to contend with!"

We zoomed right past the village of Shungnak. A little farther downstream, Don looked us in the eye, smiled knowingly, and said: "Wait 'til we get to the Black River . . ."

"What's at the Black River?" I asked.

"Oh . . . *You'll* see!" he replied. And both he and Thomas burst out laughing.

Cindy and I looked at each other ruefully. In our heads we were playing our own Arctic versions of *Deliverance*.

Thomas kept staring at Cindy. Finally, he said: "You look like kay-roo."

"What?" Cindy asked.

"You look like *kay-rooo*."

After a few more rounds of this, it finally dawned on me that Thomas was talking about Kay Rue, the wife of Dave Rue, the bush pilot in Ambler.

Cindy reached into her bottomless reserves of charm and before long she had us all in stitches. The rum continued to flow as we motored on down the river. From time to time one of our companions would return to that ominous refrain: "Wait 'til we get to the Black River . . ."

Trying to ascertain what terrible fate might await us at this dark-sounding place, Cindy and I would once again take the bait.

"Why? What's at the Black River?"

Each time the answer was the same: a mysterious "You'll see!!!" followed by uproarious laughter.

Finally, just below the mouth of a small tributary, we slowed down and pulled over to a sandbar. With a tone of gravitas, Don said: "The Black River . . ."

By now the three of us guys were pretty drunk. As we clambered out of the boat, Don said: "Okay. Everybody get sticks. We're gonna make a fire."

In a few minutes we had a small blaze going. Thomas produced a coffeepot and some coarse-ground coffee beans. When the water was hot, he threw several heaping handfuls into the pot. "Eskimo coffee," he said proudly as he poured out four cups. The black sludge tasted terrific. And it had the desired effect. Within fifteen minutes we were stone sober.

We got back on the river. A few miles farther downstream we stopped at a fish camp. At the top of a steep bank stood a large canvas-wall tent, surrounded by drying racks covered with salmon and sheefish carcasses. Inside the tent Thomas and Don introduced us to their relatives—grandparents, parents, aunts and uncles, grandchildren. We shared dried fish, seal meat, tea, and conversation. Cindy and I told them about her young son, and our lives in Fairbanks. They told us all about their families and their lives here in the Kobuk River country. By the time we left the fish camp and motored on into Ambler, the four of us were famous friends. As Thomas and Don shoved off for their return to Kobuk, we all hugged and promised we'd see one another again, in Fairbanks or maybe out here on the river. Sadly, we never did.

Don died a couple of winters later in an airplane crash at

Shungnak (the same crash of which my friend Mary Pat was the only survivor). And one summer Thomas's boat was discovered circling in the river. His body was never found. But that day we waved heartily as Don and Thomas disappeared upstream. Then, before starting up the Ambler River with Molly and Wilbur, Cindy and I paid a quick visit to see Kay Rue. To our eyes, she looked nothing at all like Cindy.

When Cindy and I first got together, her son, Sage, was just two and a half years old. For a couple of years, we lived together in a series of funky cabins around the outskirts of Fairbanks. We were working long, hard hours for marginal pay. Our living conditions—with wood heat and no running water—weren't easy. With Sage's biological father out of the picture, Cindy was fiercely protective of her son. And I—still in my twenties, haunted by the legacy of my own troubled childhood, with no good model of how to be a parent—was ill prepared for the challenges of an instant family. Eventually I moved out. Cindy took the position of executive director of the Alaska Center for the Environment, in Anchorage. Yet in spite of our difficulties, both she and I were unwilling to let each other go. And even before she left Fairbanks, we asserted our determination to somehow continue as a couple.

During my years as an activist I'd learned how to project a confident public persona. But it exhausted me. My relationship had suffered. My music had suffered. My health began to suffer. And in time I came to understand that, fundamentally, I'm an introvert. It became clear that I had to make the choice between politics and music. I chose music. Now I retreated to a cabin in the woods, where I took the passion that I felt for Alaska together with my hopes for changing the world, and put them into my art. This is the path I've followed ever since.

Today Alaska is still the youngest state in the United States, and the second-richest state. But in education it's fallen to the middle of the pack. And as Alaska has become more populous and less educated, the tenor of life in the state has changed. Big Oil has expanded and strengthened its stranglehold on the economy and the government of Alaska. Every Alaskan man, woman, and child receives an annual oil royalty check, while year after year the legislature continues to dismantle public education and social services as wild-eyed proposals for oil drilling, pipelines, mines, dams, and highways continue to proliferate. Beyond this, Alaska is threatened in a way that my young friends and I never dreamed of. Global warming has affected Alaska sooner and more dramatically than almost any other place on earth. And the wild country that we thought we had protected in 1980 is now threatened by carbon emissions from the other side of the world.

Many years later, on a lovely summer evening under the midnight sun, Cindy and I were heading back out to our home in the Goldstream Valley, after an Alaska Goldpanners baseball game. She was driving. The home team had won. But as we rumbled over the Chena River bridge on University Avenue, I looked out the window and (apropos of nothing in particular) casually remarked: "We lost."

"Yep," she replied.

No further discussion was necessary. Both of us knew what we meant.

| II |

My Own Private Walden

I came to this place,
a young man green and lonely.
—JOHN HAINES

During my early years in Fairbanks I lived in a series of cabins, first alone on Farmer's Loop Road, and then with Cindy and Sage—on Grenac Road, the Old Steese Highway, and on a hillside in the Goldstream Valley. But Cindy and I were having difficulty adjusting to living together, and I moved out to a tiny place high up on Ester Dome. (To the north, Fairbanks is ringed by what might be called mountains in New England but what, with Denali visible to the southwest, locals refer to as "domes.") Gordon knew all about my domestic problems, and one evening after rehearsal with the Fairbanks Symphony he said to me matter-of-factly: "You and I are going to be next-door neighbors. Tomorrow I'm going to take you to the cabin you're going to buy."

A few years earlier, Gordon's marriage had come apart. He moved out of the family house in the suburbs and found a small cabin in the woods a few miles west of the university (and about ten miles from downtown). The area was known as Findlay Forest, after Findlay Abbott, who had homesteaded 160 acres of spruce woods, then divided it up and given most of it away to his friends with the dream of creating a kind of Alaskan Ecotopia.

The forest is almost entirely underlain with permafrost, so none of the cabins have running water, and there's no year-round road. Everyone parks in a gravel lot near the road to town and hikes in to their places. Farthest back in the woods, a mile and a half from the road, stood the cabin of a couple of young Alaska

dreamers, Dan and Helen Adams. Dan had built the cabin himself, hauling the materials in by sled and on his back. Now, preparing for the arrival of their first baby, they'd decided it was
time to move out of the spruce bog and up onto the ridge somewhere. So they were selling "the Adams Place."

Dan and Helen said they'd be happy to pass it along to another Adams for whatever the appraised value might be. That
sounded fair. The appraisal came in at $42,500, for a rambling
cabin and five acres of stunted forest. That was a lot of money to
me. But it might have been substantially more if the appraiser
hadn't declared the property "functionally obsolete." The report
defined the term this way: "Functional obsolescence is the inabil-
ity of a property to perform the function for which it is intended.
The subject property is impaired by lack of convenient access, and
therefore indicates functional obsolescence." As I read this, my
heart swelled with backwoods pride. And for years this declara-
tion hung prominently on the wall above my desk.

My cabin was deep in the black spruce bog. The nicer houses
around Fairbanks are on the hilltops and the south-facing slopes
with views of the Alaska Range. Up there it's much warmer in
winter, and you get every precious minute of sunlight. Down
in the bog the only view was the forest, and it was often 20 degrees colder than the higher elevations. For several weeks each
winter I got no direct sunlight at my cabin. The day in January
when the sun returned to the south-facing picture window was
always a big moment. Although they had the view, the light, and
the relative warmth, we bog-dwellers looked down on those soft-
ies up on the hillsides. We had more space, a lot fewer people,
and a lot more wildlife. Our day-to-day life was much closer to
the earth. And I wouldn't have had it any other way.

The Russian word for this forest is *taiga*, which translates
literally as "little sticks." The trees are old, but they don't look

that way. They're stunted and spindly because they're growing on top of permafrost—permanently frozen ground. In winter the ground beneath my cabin was solid as bedrock. But in summer it was a little like living on a houseboat. Instead of a conventional foundation or pilings, my house rested on a rim of creosote-soaked railroad ties lying in the muck. Each spring when the surface began to thaw, I would break out my bubble level, a bucket full of shims, and a small hydraulic jack to level up the house. First I would check to see which way the ship was listing. Then I would jack it up and add or remove a few shims here and there. I would continue this all the way around the perimeter. If I didn't perform this annual maintenance, within a few years the windows would be cracked, the doors would be jammed shut, and my cabin would begin to break apart and sink into the spongy, saturated ground.

Since the permafrost made it impossible to drill a well or to bury a water tank, I lived without running water. In the spring and the summer, I collected snowmelt and rainwater from the roof in big barrels. I took showers in town at the laundromat, or bathed in the sauna. I carried my drinking water into the cabin in jugs. My privy was an outhouse. The toilet was a wooden box topped with thick Styrofoam—a great comfort on cold winter nights. Because of the permafrost, I couldn't dig a deep hole. So my throne sat on top of a cardboard box lined with a heavy plastic garbage bag. When the bag was full, I would simply tie it up, remove the frozen block, and add a fresh liner to the box. In the summertime I would take the bag into the woods, peel back the moss, and bury the contents. It was impossible to have a garden on that frozen ground, so I kept a small, rough greenhouse in which I did my best to raise a few tomatoes, peppers, and some lettuce. But it was a far cry from my glory days as a vegetable gardener in Georgia.

Not far from my cabin was a lovely little lake. From there it was a short way through the woods to another, larger lake. Some uninspired poet named these Ace Lake and Deuce Lake. But they're jewels in the forest, and over the years I enjoyed many long walks and moonlit skis around them.

The furnishings in my cabin were Spartan. Near the center of the main room stood the woodstove. There was one large but very plain table, and a single chair, where I ate and worked. Nestled in one corner was my Fender Rhodes electric piano (which a year or two later I'd replace with a battered baby grand). The only other furniture was a small couch, where I sat to read or occasionally visit with Gordon. From time to time John Haines or another overnight guest would sleep there. I had an old windup clock, which ticked loudly. I resented the sound. And I didn't want to be watching the clock, or to feel that the clock was watching me. So I kept it in the refrigerator. If I really needed to know the time, I had to make a conscious decision to walk into the kitchen area, open the door, and peer in among the fruits and vegetables.

Sometimes, when I was composing, my cabin felt like a monk's cell. At other times, especially when Cindy and I were having trouble in our relationship, it could feel more like a jail cell. But that cabin was my refuge. I remember coming home late one winter evening. I'd had a long day at my job, followed by three hours of orchestra rehearsal, and then I had to fight just to make my way down the trail through the deep snow and the bitter cold.

At last I stepped inside. I closed the door, laid my pack down, and sank back with a deep sigh of relief:

"Ahhh . . . Sweet austerity!"

Gordon's cabin was half a mile from mine. But he and I weren't the only ones living out here in the woods. Nearby in an underground sod igloo lived Robert Drozda, a cultural anthropologist who spent a lot of time out on Nunivak Island in the Bering Sea, working with the Yup'ik people there to create a map of traditional geographic place-names. John Kristopeit, a wildlife biology student at the university, lived in another small cabin, and in yet another was Anne-Linne Rochet, a quiet Frenchwoman who had fled Paris and her family, and now made her living harvesting mushrooms, herbs, and wild berries throughout the interior of Alaska. Frank and Nora Foster had lived in these woods longer than anyone. Nora was a researcher at the Institute of Marine Biology at the University of Alaska, and Frank worked as a sanitation engineer at what he called the "Poop Plant" in downtown Fairbanks.

Along the edge of our "neighborhood" ran a trail called the Dredge Swath, which had been cut to haul dredges between the gold mine near Ester and those along Goldstream Creek to the north. Running down the center of this trail for well over a mile was a beautifully built and meticulously maintained boardwalk. This was Frank's pride and joy. Because I took a more direct route through the woods to my cabin, I didn't use the boardwalk on a daily basis. But often in summer I'd walk that way just to enjoy the smooth cushiony feeling and the sound of my rubber boots on the wood.

One afternoon I ran into Frank in the parking lot. Frank was always supportive of my music, and so when he told me he'd like to commission a new piece, I took the bait.

"Really?" I asked. "What do you have in mind?"

"I'd like you to do a panel for the boardwalk."

I knew I was hooked, and I readily agreed.

A few days later I came home to find oil paints in several colors, brushes in several sizes, and a precut section of boardwalk waiting on the deck of my cabin—everything I needed to fulfill my commission. It was springtime, and the forest was filled with music. So I painted a musical staff with a couple of phrases from my favorite singers with the title *Hermit Thrushes in the Forest*.

Frank maintained the boardwalk for anyone and everyone who might want to use it. Many years later, he died with his boots on—working on the boardwalk.

Shortly after I had moved to Fairbanks, Gordon informed me that I was going to play timpani with the Fairbanks Symphony and the Arctic Chamber Orchestra. This idea didn't especially appeal to me. I was working overtime as an activist, and settling into a new relationship with Cindy. I had little interest in most orchestral music. So, for a couple of years, I resisted Gordon's persistent campaign of conscription. But eventually, perhaps inevitably, I relented.

What finally persuaded me was a sort of devil's bargain: if I would play in his orchestras, Gordon would perform my music. There's no doubt that I got the better end of this deal. But Gordon held up his end faithfully and with genuine conviction for the rest of his life.

Although I'd never played timpani, I was a percussionist of sorts and I knew how to read a score. Besides, if Gordon believed I could do it, then who was I to doubt? I ordered some mallets by mail and began practicing. Since I lived out in the woods and didn't have free access to the timpani at the university, I did a lot of my practicing at home in my cabin, where my "drums" were four pillows from the sofa.

My first concert with the Fairbanks Symphony included *Credendum* by William Schuman, which has a big flashy timpani solo. I practiced diligently on my pillow drums, and at the first rehearsal I nailed the part. Some of the musicians in the orchestra applauded. My fate was sealed, and for the next decade or so, I was Gordon's timpanist.

Gordon was my best friend. Yet whenever he was on the podium and I was behind the drums, he always addressed me as "Timpani." Calling me by the name of my instrument made it clear that the work at hand was not personal. This was not about *us*. It was about the music.

At one of my early rehearsals, I took my one and only unauthorized timpani solo. We were reading through Beethoven's *Eroica* Symphony for the first time. At the beginning of the final movement, there's a moment when the orchestra tattoos a unison rhythm, followed by silence. I spaced out and I fell behind by a couple of beats.

The orchestra played: *Bum-bum BUM . . .*

And the drums answered boldly: *Boom-boom BOOM . . . !*

Gordon stopped and looked at me.

"Timpani," he said with mock empathy, "you're allowed to do that . . ." He paused for dramatic effect before adding emphatically, *"Once!"*

Everyone burst out laughing. I tried to disappear beneath the drums. And I never played in a rest again.

In time I became a fairly good timpanist, maybe better than I'd been as a rock drummer. I relished the big timpani parts in Beethoven, Brahms, Mahler, and Sibelius. I remember how proud I was when I managed to play the fiendishly difficult chromatic passage for timpani in the fourth movement of the Bartok *Concerto for Orchestra*. The key was to sit on a stool, remove my shoes, and play the quick pedal changes in my sock feet.

Under Gordon's direction, the Fairbanks Symphony played

lots of music that by all rights should've been beyond the capabilities of a volunteer orchestra on the edge of nowhere. But in typical Alaskan spirit, we didn't care. We fearlessly tackled anything that appeared on our music stands. "The world's scrappiest orchestra," Gordon called us.

Over the course of the years, Gordon led me on a never-ending quest for his ideal timpani sound. Riffing on the German word for kettledrums, he called this elusive Holy Grail *Pauke* (pronounced POWK!).

We were rehearsing the Bach Mass in B Minor when Gordon implored: "Timpani, I need more *Pauke!*"

I tried harder mallets. The Maestro wasn't satisfied.

"More *Pauke!*"

I pulled out the hardest mallets I had. Still, Gordon wanted more, exhorting me: "It should sound like socking a cow in the belly!"

So I turned my mallets over and used the wooden butts.

Gordon loved the sound! And I played the entire Mass in B Minor with the wrong end of the sticks.

Gordon called me the "second conductor," and I took this seriously. Not only did I learn my timpani parts, I also studied the scores of the major pieces we played. I came to know a lot of great music that previously (with my modern-music myopia) I'd snobbishly avoided. And in the process, I learned a great deal about large-scale form and about orchestration, which has served me well in my own work as a composer.

I'd moved to the woods and left the Environmental Center determined to rededicate myself to my music. But I still needed an income. Someone told me there was an opening at the local public radio station. I had no real experience in radio. I'd been interviewed about my music, now and then. I could write a little. I knew something about both classical and popular music.

People told me I had a clear, distinctive voice. Besides, I met the most important qualification in Alaska in those days: I was *there*.

Over the next seven years I worked at KUAC-FM in various capacities. At first I was the afternoon host on weekends. Then I became the music director. Toward the end of my tenure I became program director. But the pinnacle of my radio days was the weekly program I produced titled simply *The New Music*. I played music by Charles Ives, Edgard Varèse, Ruth Crawford Seeger, and Harry Partch. I played Pauline Oliveros and James Tenney. I played Meredith Monk, Philip Glass, and Steve Reich. I played works by Lois V. Vierk, Jim Fox, Peter Garland, and other composers of my generation. In time I began doing interviews with composers, at first by telephone and later in person. In the years that I produced *The New Music* I recorded conversations with Dane Rudhyar, Conlon Nancarrow, Morton Feldman, Lou Harrison, Glenn Branca, Robert Ashley, James Tenney, and many others.

Each year during the on-air fundraising drive, my program received more listener comments than any program aside from the big NPR flagship shows. The comments usually ran about fifty-fifty pro and con. Some people loved it. Other people hated it. Among my favorite comments were those from listeners who said they'd hated it at first, but had begun to like some of this weird new music. Even better were the comments from people who said they hated the show but were happy it was on the air.

As I settled into life in the forest, Gordon and I established a regular ritual. Every Sunday evening, at his cabin, we shared a sauna followed by dinner. By the time I arrived, around 6:30, Gordon usually had the sauna hot. We'd sweat for an hour or so, then adjourn to the cabin to finish cooking and then to dine, sip scotch, and continue talking. Our conversations were wide-ranging—the miracles of music, the mysteries of women, the conundrum of politics, the geography of Alaska, and the meaning of existence. Often, we'd read aloud to each other, sharing poems, amusements, or profundities we'd come across in our individual reading.

The conversation at the sauna was different from our conversations on camping trips, on tour with the Arctic Chamber Orchestra, or in our day-to-day work together. At the sauna things were relaxed and wide open. Yet there was also a kind of formality to the proceedings. In that small space our friendship deepened. Some of the most meaningful conversations Gordon and I shared were in the sauna.

In time Gordon and I invited other friends to join us on Sunday evenings. First was Birch Pavelsky, the carpenter-poet. Birch builds exquisite log cabins, often in remote locations. He works alone, and refuses to use power tools. A similar devotion to making beautiful things informs the poems he writes, as does his concern about the state of human affairs and his love for Alaska. Once, when I asked Birch, "Do you ever think about leaving Alaska?" he answered me with a question: "Where would I go?" Then he added: "Alaska is my fate."

Next to join us was Dietrich Strohmaier, a reflective, well-read surveyor who'd come north in the late 1940s, before Alaska was a state. Gordon dubbed us the Ace Lake Sauna Society, after the lake in the woods beyond my cabin. Over the years we acquired other members, including the philosopher-fisherman John Kooistra, and the musician-physician Leif Thompson.

After earning a graduate degree in music in California with the aspiration to become a composer, Leif had returned to Alaska and begun working as a wilderness guide. Several years of that convinced him that he preferred to travel in wild country without being responsible for other people. So Leif went back to school in Oregon and eventually returned home as a family physician (with his long, red braided ponytail) and became active as a folk musician.

A professor of philosophy at the University of Alaska, John Kooistra had left academia to become a commercial fisherman, and to build his own house, largely alone. In the years since selling his boat, John has lived frugally and traveled widely. Like Birch, John also writes poetry, informed by a gentle sense of detachment and humor as dry as the fine wines he favors.

There was a lot of flannel at the sauna, but there were a variety of views on the relative merits of other elements of the winter wardrobe. Birch favored insulated Carhartts. I preferred zip-up snowmobile overalls. Leif was an early adopter of synthetic fleece, but John Kooistra tended toward goose down. Ever the traditionalist, Gordon wore wool mittens, while I wore oversize synthetic mittens with silk or cotton liners. Birch and Gordon swore by the Norwegian wool boots called *lobben*. But as stylish as they are, when the temperature dropped much below zero my feet were always cold in those. And once I switched over to moosehide *mukluks* with felt liners, my *lobben* were rarely seen again.

We all sported large beards, which were eminently practical during the harsh winters, and proud expressions of our identities as woodsy Alaskans. Sometime in the nineties, I saw a photograph of myself and realized that I was a pretty scary-looking character who wouldn't have seemed out of place on the "Most Wanted" board at the local post office. So I trimmed my beard down to a fairly close crop. When I arrived at the sauna that evening, Gordon took one look at me and harrumphed: "Well, you might as well not even *have* a beard . . ."

From time to time we'd host visiting dignitaries—guest soloists with the Fairbanks Symphony, the writer Barry Lopez, and

Alaska's great poet, John Haines. John was well into his eighties when I finally persuaded him to join us at the sauna. It was minus 40 degrees that night, and about halfway into the walk to Gordon's cabin I became seriously concerned that we might lose John to hypothermia. I could just see the headlines in the *Fairbanks Daily News-Miner*: "Local Composer Kills Poet Laureate in Pagan Rite." But the poet survived, and we all had another story to tell.

The sauna sits thirty or forty yards behind Gordon's cabin. On the deck of the cabin stood the pile of wood for daily use, neatly cut to fit into the stove. All around the cabin were Gordon's meticulous stacks of larger wood—eighteen-inch rounds of spruce and birch. It was these woodpiles that we used for the sauna. In front of the cabin was an especially stout butt of spruce. Here, with a splitting maul, we quartered the larger pieces of wood. Then for kindling we took an axe to the quarters.

Inside the cabin we would pour water out of a five-gallon jug into a bucket that we'd carry out to the sauna. Sometimes we would fill this bucket with snow and place it on the sauna stove. We would leave our clothes in the cabin and walk to the sauna stark naked or wrapped in towels. In winter I would wear the worn-out slippers that sat under the ladder to Gordon's loft. The soles were treacherously slick, but they kept my feet relatively warm, and they became part of my regular sauna routine. In summer I'd walk barefoot—the cold, wet muck from the trail squishing between my toes.

The rough frame structure is small, not more than ten feet long and maybe seven feet wide. There's a small covered deck where we would stack wood and stash our water and beers to keep them cold and close at hand. The door is small and very low. Gordon had to fold his six-foot-seven frame and get on his hands and knees to enter. The roof is low, not tall enough for a man to stand upright, even at the ridgeline.

Inside are two low benches. The longer of these is just long enough and wide enough for me to lie down. But when the heat was intense, I'd usually wind up lying on the floor. The stove is an old oil drum fitted with an iron door and wrapped with large stones to hold the heat. From a heavy hook in the ceiling we would hang a metal sprinkler can filled with water. This was our shower. We'd also use it to rain water over the hot stones, filling the room with scalding steam. We kept a bucket handy, too, and a large ladle. Sometimes we would add a few drops of eucalyptus oil to the water and ladle it on for a blast of aromatic vapor. There were also cedar and sage bundles, which we occasionally used when we felt moved to spread the fragrant smoke over our bodies.

At first, we favored the Finnish-style dry sauna. But after I visited the Aleutian Islands and shared a searing steam bath with Native men out there, I craved a more intense experience. From then on we'd begin our sweat with dry heat, switching to steam after a while. From the Aleutians I'd brought back a traditional grass switch that a friend there made for me. There was also a bald eagle feather that we sometimes employed for lighter flagellation. During a typical session we'd be in and out of the sauna two or three times, to cool down. Once in a while, amid wild exclamations, we would throw ourselves into the snow. This invariably made my skin tingle in a way that my brain couldn't decode. Were all those pinpricks hot or cold?

Each session in the sauna was unique. The experience varied with the season, the weather, the size and makeup of the group, how we were feeling physically, and what was on our minds. Sometimes the conversation was quiet and reflective. Other times it was stream of consciousness, off-the-wall and boisterous, filled with good-natured joking at one another's expense. But invariably we would return to the cabin limp and glowing, ready for dinner, reading, and libations.

At these gatherings, usually after sauna and before dinner, Gordon—our unanimously anointed benevolent despot—would convene an ersatz business meeting. During these sessions we discussed matters of grave import. Would we take a stand on the situation in Eastern Europe? When and where would we get our next load of firewood? Who would bring dessert to the next meeting? And who would bring the beer?

For several years we had regular beer tastings in the sauna. Each week one of the crew would be the designated host, to present a flight of brews around a theme of his choosing. One week I might present Belgian ales. The next week, Leif might present West Coast microbrews. After that John Kristopeit would treat us to French *lambics*, or ales of the British Isles. But the most memorable evening by far was Gordon's presentation of a "swill tasting."

In those days, when fancy beers invariably came in a bottle, the host proclaimed proudly: "Nothing in a bottle. Cans only."

Our beer tastings were "blind," with all beverages presented in brown paper bags. One by one, each bottle (or can) was passed around the sauna. Commentary was offered. And after a second round of tasting, we rated each numerically—from 0 to 10—tallied up the scores, took the average, and declared the winner. Gordon presented some astonishing brews that evening—Schaefer, Schlitz, Pabst Blue Ribbon, Colt 45. Due to the unusual nature of this particular theme, the scoring system was inverted. The brew with the *lowest* score was proclaimed the winner. As I recall, it was Hamm's. But the standout novelty of the night was Prinz Brau, produced by a brewery in Anchorage that had gone out of business several years before. The beer had not improved with age. And it was abundantly clear why the enterprise had failed.

Another highlight of our sauna gatherings was the reading

aloud. As with the beer tastings, we rotated the curatorship. We read John Haines. Occasionally one of us would present a poem of our own. A recurring favorite of mine was to read the "Shouts and Murmurs" humor column from *The New Yorker*. But the literary patron saint of the Ace Lake Sauna Society was Ambrose Bierce.

We had an edition of *The Complete Works of Ambrose Bierce* that Gordon had picked up in a used-book store. We called it "the Good Book," and we read from it at almost every gathering. When we were short on time, we'd read a few brief selections from *Fantastic Fables* or *The Devil's Dictionary*. Gordon had little use for either church or state. To his delight, Bierce spared neither:

> CHRISTIAN, n. One who believes that the New Testament is a divinely inspired book admirably suited to the spiritual needs of his neighbor. One who follows the teachings of Christ in so far as they are not inconsistent with a life of sin.

> ALLEGIANCE, n.
> This thing Allegiance, as I suppose,
> Is a ring fitted in the subject's nose,
> Whereby that organ is kept rightly pointed
> To smell the sweetness of the Lord's anointed.

Over the years, we worked our way through most of the Bierce canon, including the bizarre novella *The Monk and the Hangman's Daughter*. The perennial favorite was "Oil of Dog," a short story from the collection titled *The Parenticide Club*. The first time Gordon read it aloud with mock solemnity ("My name is Boffer Biggs . . ."), I snorted and belly laughed until it hurt.

Time and again we returned to that chilling tale of boiling pets
and parents in oil.

I'd come to Alaska with an English setter–German shepherd
mix who might've been a suitable candidate for the oil vats of
Boffer Biggs. Rascal lived up to his name. He was unfriendly to
everyone except his owner. He lived with Cindy, Sage, and me
in the cabin on the Old Steese Highway. And when our next-
door neighbor's chickens began disappearing, Rascal also disappeared. Although we were never sure exactly what happened to
him, we had a pretty good idea. But Rascal had the last laugh.
A few weeks after he vanished, the neighbor's dog gave birth
to a whole litter of little Rascals. One of those puppies was Pogo,
the dog of my lifetime.

As sweet as his father had been cranky, he was my loyal companion for thirteen years. Always formally attired in his smooth
black coat and gleaming white shirt, Pogo was a regular fixture
at our Sunday-night saunas, curling up contentedly on the rug
while the boys carried on. Pogo loved everybody. And everybody
loved Pogo. Gordon called Pogo his Zen master.

As Pogo got old and sickly, Gordon sensed that he wasn't long
for this world. So before leaving town to return to his cabin on
Turnagain Arm, he came up to our house on Coyote Trail to
say goodbye. Gordon lay down on the floor and pressed his nose
against Pogo's nose, looked into his eyes, and whispered softly
to him. After Pogo died, we had a little ceremony for him in the
sauna. Gordon told us that our challenge now was to find "the
Pogo within."

In 1989 Gordon retired from the symphony and the university, and moved from Fairbanks to his new cabin in the Chugach
Mountains, south of Anchorage. He talked seriously about selling the cabin in the forest. But I protested so vociferously that he
kept it. A couple of times each year he would come up for a week

or two, and we would convene the old crew for a sauna. Although
the meetings now are fewer and farther between, whenever I'm in
Alaska we still fire up the stove, and the Ace Lake Sauna Society
has continued through its fourth decade.

After so many years I've come to know this small space as
well as any in my life—as well as I know my studio, and better
than I've known my own houses. Birch calls it "the Navel of the
Universe." In some ways I feel safer and more at ease here than
anyplace else. Once when I'd been away for a long time, traveling
far and wide, I crawled into the sauna. Birch was already inside.
As I sat down, quietly and knowingly he said: "It's okay, John.
You can breathe now."

Aside from Gordon, whom I saw daily, I glimpsed most of my
human neighbors less frequently than I encountered moose on
the trail. My closest other-than-human neighbors included the
weasel that lived in one of my woodpiles, the flying squirrel that
occasionally startled me by swooping down and sticking to the
side of my cabin, and the great horned owl that sat right outside my window one evening and watched me as I ate my entire
dinner. (Not wanting to disturb him, but needing to leave for
orchestra rehearsal, I tiptoed out the back door.) But my most
ubiquitous and animated neighbors were the red squirrels.

Sometime in the early eighties, Gordon and I team-taught a
course in twentieth-century music history at the University of
Alaska Fairbanks. Gordon handled the first half of the century,
with a focus more on the European side of things. I took over
about 1950, with a decidedly American experimentalist bias. The
students were a bright and lively bunch. Among them was the
shy but very inquisitive Leif Thompson. At the time I was all
of twenty-nine or thirty, which would've made Leif eighteen or

nineteen. Leif quickly became enamored of the music of Cage, Partch, Feldman, and many others of my favorite composers. Not surprisingly, he and I became friends outside of class, and I invited him to visit me at my cabin in the bog.

In those days I observed a macrobiotic diet. (A problematic proposition in the subarctic, to say the least. But that's a different story.) And I lived alone . . . except for the squirrels. My cabin was fairly infested with them. They nested throughout the walls and ceiling, where they rearranged the fiberglass insulation, birthed their young, stored their winter caches of spruce cones, and woke me up at all hours of the night.

I nailed fine-mesh metal screen under the eaves all around the house. But the squirrels managed to eat their way around the screen and back in. I ignored this for as long as I could. Then I begrudgingly tolerated it. Eventually I could no longer deny that I had a serious problem. The squirrels were quite literally eating my house. But, committed pacifist that I was (and still am), I needed to find a nonviolent solution. I called the Alaska Department of Fish and Game. A nice woman there told me I could borrow a "live trap" from them. This turned out to be a small cage with a spring-loaded door and a convenient handle for carrying the unwelcome rodents to another location. The brand name was Havahart.

For more than a year, winter and summer, I trapped squirrels. Maybe they were following the macrobiotic diet, too. In any case they were suckers for crunchy unhydrogenated peanut butter on brown rice cakes. I'd set the bait and within an hour I'd have a squirrel. Each time I'd carry the laden Havahart out to my car, drive twenty or thirty miles (toward Nenana, or North Pole, or Fox), and release my quarry, unharmed. No sooner was I back home than, invariably, a new squirrel would appear. In another day or two I'd reload and trap the next squirrel. Or was it the same one? I sometimes wondered whether I simply trapped the same squirrel over and over again.

Maybe red squirrels have an irrepressible homing instinct. Or perhaps the woods around my cabin had an effectively inexhaustible population of the bushy-tailed rodents. Who knows how many times I performed this senseless ritual?

The cycle might well have continued ad infinitum. But one night I was sitting at the piano, deep into composing, when I was startled from my musings by a rude chattering—like the sound of a highly amplified ratchet. And it was in the room with me.

RRRRRRRRRRRRRRRRRRRRRRRRRRRRR!!!!!!!!

"What are you doing in *my* house? And what the hell is that noise you're making?" he seemed to say.

Something inside me snapped. I leaped to my feet, waved my arms wildly, and fired a geyser of hostile profanity at the intruder. Enough was enough.

The next day I went to see the only person I knew who owned a gun—John Haines. Out at his homestead on the Richardson Highway, John showed me how to load and fire a little .22-caliber rifle. I took it home, put it in the Arctic entryway of my cabin, and waited.

It didn't take long. The next afternoon I was working at the piano when I heard chattering and rustling in the entryway. I opened the door. There sat what I took to be the same brazen squirrel that had read me the riot act from the top of my refrigerator. I chased him out, but he retreated only a short distance, scurried up a tree, and began giving me unrelenting hell. So I grabbed the .22, loaded it, and walked out to the deck. I raised the gun, aimed, and fired.

Just as I did, here came young Leif innocently sauntering down the final few feet of the boardwalk to my cabin. All he heard was *Bang!* followed by my angry exclamation: "Bastard!"

The squirrel fell to the ground with a terminal *thunk.*

Leif had never been out to visit me at my cabin before. This was his introduction to the home life of his cabin-dwelling, tree-hugging, peace-talking teacher. It must have been a moment of profound disillusionment for him.

I've never owned a gun. And I doubt that I ever will. But the National Rifle Association may be right about one thing: Guns don't kill squirrels. People kill squirrels.

I confess I felt a certain macho pride that I'd dispatched my one and only squirrel with a single shot. But I also felt horrible about killing the little guy. The next day I returned the gun to John Haines, and took the Havahart trap back to Fish and Game. From that day on, I resolved that the house belonged to the squirrels. They merely allowed me to sleep, eat, and sometimes work there.

Years later I told this story in the sauna. Birch responded with a story of his own.

Birch had gone out to do some carpentry work at the John Haines homestead. John was away, but he had left a note for Birch outlining the work to be done, and asking Birch to dispatch a squirrel that had been wreaking havoc in the entryway to John's cabin.

Birch did the dirty deed, and left this note for Haines:

> John,
> Shot the squirrel. Tried to charge it on your karmic
> account, but it was overdrawn. So I put it on Adams.
> Birch

Little did Birch suspect that Adams already had a fair amount of squirrel karma drawn against his own account.

In the winter of 1980–81 I received in the mail an envelope with a familiar return address, "Mile 68 Richardson Highway"—the

John Haines homestead. Inside were drafts of a new cycle of poems. In the accompanying note John asked whether I might find
something musical in them.

My response was immediate and enthusiastic: "Yes!"

Not long afterward, John and I met at my cabin one evening
to discuss our nascent collaboration. John brought with him a
bottle of the Hungarian red wine Egri Bikavér—"Bull's Blood."
Although we made quick work of its contents, I kept that bottle
as a kind of talisman. Even now, holding it in my hand, I can
almost touch the excitement I felt on that evening in the forest,
so long ago.

The work that took shape over that bottle of wine was *Forest
Without Leaves*—a cantata for choir, vocal soloists, and chamber
orchestra. The fifteen poems of John's cycle address the inextri-
cable ties between human beings and the natural world, from
prehistory to postapocalypse. Once we had an outline, I took
the idea to Gordon, who readily agreed to premiere the piece
with the Arctic Chamber Orchestra. Soon, thanks to the active
support of the poet Gary Holthaus (who was then serving as
executive director of the Alaska Humanities Forum), we found
funding for the project.

Out of respect for John and his work, I resolved to be as faithful as possible to the natural melodic and rhythmic flow, the in-
herent music of the words. Invoking Monteverdi, Mussorgsky, and
Partch as models, I wrote:

> Any composer who sets out to add tones to a text of
> integrity faces a formidable challenge. As language, the
> words are complete in and of themselves. Yet when they
> are spoken, their inherent music seems to cry out for the
> added resonance of singing voices and instruments. The
> composer's challenge, then, is to enhance that inherent

music without impairing the imagery or meanings of the words. This demands a serious obligation of fidelity to words not only as sound, but as language. The common conventions of "setting words to music"—forcing them into rigid meters, formulaic harmonies, architectural forms, and essentially instrumental melodies—are simply inappropriate. Instead, the composer must search for the music within the words . . . The natural flow of their rhythms and the curves of their melodies should be the seeds from which everything grows. Their integrity as language should always be respected, the sound and sense always preserved.

In spite of these convictions, if I couldn't find the music in a particular poem, I felt comfortable telling John. His response was always the same: "Well, let's just leave that one out." In one instance, I wanted to keep the poem but leave out a middle stanza. That was fine with John, too. And if a specific phrase or word didn't work for me, John was perfectly willing to consider another.

As I was working with one of the loveliest poems in *Forest Without Leaves*, I kept stumbling over one particular line. I asked John whether he might consider an alternative to the word *clod*.

"I just can't make it sing," I said. "Would you consider changing it to *cloud*?"

This was no trivial request. In essence I was asking the poet to move heaven and earth. To my surprise, he agreed instantly, and the line became:

And sometimes through the air,
this dust is like a willow
tethered to a cloud.

And it appears in this form in John's collected poems.

The work flowed easily, back and forth between us. During my days at the Environmental Center, I hadn't composed as much as I'd wanted. Working on *Forest Without Leaves*, I began to feel like a composer again. I composed much of the music in my cabin, at the keyboard of that Fender Rhodes. Things evolved slowly and painstakingly, as I worked syllable by syllable, to hear and augment the natural prosody of John's poems. But there were occasional moments of grace.

One evening, leaving my late shift at the local public radio station and walking through the hallways of the Fine Arts Complex, I passed by the stage door of the concert hall. It was closed, but not locked. I stepped inside, turned up the lights, and walked onto the stage. There stood the beautiful nine-foot Steinway. It, too, was unlocked. I sat down and lifted the keyboard cover.

My right thumb touched middle C. Gently, I struck it. The sound and the feel of the instrument were rich and supple, so unlike the heavy metallic clunk and ping of my electric instrument at home. I began to trace a simple arpeggio, expanding up and down . . .

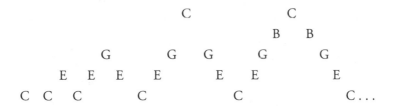

I stopped and pulled my sketchbook, a pencil, and one of John's poems out of my pack.

> How the sun came to the forest
> How the rain spoke
> and the green branch flowered . . .

The melody began to flow from the words and an hour later I had completed "How the Sun Came to the Forest," for sopranos, altos, alto flute, English horn, harp, and strings.

The poem is one of the most lyrical in all of John's work. And if there's a "hit single" in *Forest Without Leaves*, this is it. When he first heard the piece, Birch said: "This should be the state song for the new Alaska."

Birch was one of the twenty-four similarly generous-spirited friends who gave voice to *Forest Without Leaves*. There was no standing choral ensemble in Fairbanks that was up for the job, so I recruited my own group of select volunteers. The long-suffering singers indulged me as I tried out new musical ideas and improved my conducting technique at their expense, all the while demanding obsessive accuracy of rhythm and clarity of diction. I was determined that every syllable of every one of John's words would be heard and understood by our audience. Although it was difficult for me to let go, in the final week before the premiere, I relinquished the podium to a veteran choral conductor from San Francisco.

Forest Without Leaves generated a lot of local interest. There were big feature stories in the Anchorage and Fairbanks newspapers, as well as radio and print interviews. The unabashedly ecocentric perspective of John's poems did not reflect the views of many of our neighbors. Even so, on November 11, 1984, the Davis Concert Hall at the University of Alaska Fairbanks was full.

Before the performance, the distinguished writer Barry Lopez addressed the audience, speaking for a few minutes about the larger themes of *Forest Without Leaves*. I had never met Barry, but I'd admired his work since the early seventies, when I first encountered it in the pages of *Audubon* magazine. His book *Desert Notes* had been in my backpack alongside John's *Winter News* during my first summer traveling in the Arctic. His *Arctic Dreams*, which appeared two years later, became a touchstone for me. Over the years, Barry and I have worked together on several projects. And by now he is one of my oldest and closest friends.

In 1984 the coffers of the State of Alaska were overflowing with money from the Trans-Alaska Pipeline, and the legislature was hell-bent on building new roads, ports, dams, pipelines, and refineries all over the state. The Soviet Union had not yet fallen. Ronald Reagan had just been reelected for his second term as president, and a full-blown expansion of the military was underway. A big new infantry unit and the "Star Wars" missile system were soon to be based in Alaska. There was not yet widespread recognition of global warming. Nuclear winter seemed a more likely end for human civilization, and the penultimate poem in *Forest Without Leaves* conjures that apocalyptic vision. Yet even amid the prospect of doom, the piece concludes on a note of faith and hope.

> A birch leaf held fast
> in limestone ten million years
> still quietly burns,
> though claimed by the darkness.
> Let earth be this windfall
> swept to a handful of seeds—
> one tree, one leaf, gives us plenty of light.

Those last two words were highlighted by two high bell tones— A-flat rising a Major Ninth to G—ringing out brightly over the full choir and orchestra.

The response of the audience was overwhelming. As John and I joined the musicians onstage to receive the ovation, someone presented us with bouquets. But these were not bouquets of flowers. They were bundles of naked birch branches tied together, from each of which hung a single birch leaf dipped in gold, with the final line of the piece inscribed on it.

A week or so after the concert in Fairbanks, we gave two more performances of *Forest* in a single day at a church in Anchorage. During a recreational ride on a dogsled in Fairbanks, our guest conductor had sustained a leg injury that required him to return to San Francisco for surgery. So I conducted. After three years of composing and a year of rehearsing the piece, I knew the score well. The choir and orchestra rose to the occasion, and I simply rode their waves.

A few weeks later we recorded *Forest*, in the concert hall in Fairbanks. The following year (1985) an LP appeared, and the Arctic Chamber Orchestra toured the piece in Switzerland, Norway, Sweden, and Finland. Gordon conducted, and I played percussion.

Forest Without Leaves was a milestone in my life. Working closely with John Haines encouraged me to think more deeply about what it meant to be an artist in the Far North, giving me the temerity to entertain artistic aspirations to match the landscapes of Alaska. What I didn't and perhaps couldn't fully appreciate at the time was just how much our collaboration meant to John. For the rest of his life he would speak frequently and wistfully of those days: "I'll always remember that big banner hanging above the Cushman Street Bridge, in letters three feet high . . ."

Forest Without Leaves
poems by John Haines
music by John Adams

I heated my cabin with wood. But the trees in our forest were too small and too precious to cut. My firewood came from wildfire salvage areas in higher, south-facing locations. Occasionally in winter, when the ground was frozen and the snow wasn't too deep, I could chain up my pickup truck and drive in over the old mining trail, carrying loads of firewood, lumber, hardware, drinking water, canned goods, and other staples. But most of the time I had to bring my wood and everything else into my cabin with the strength of my own back.

Year-round I carried an old-fashioned woven-wood trapper's pack basket, with a wooden lid and leather hinges. John Haines introduced me to this style, which is sturdy, lightweight, and easy to pack. In winter I pulled a sled, using bungee cords to keep my load in place. Although I had no regular exercise program, hiking in and out and carrying heavy loads over the rough mile and a half of trail seemed to keep me in shape.

For my first couple of years in the woods I used cheap sleds. But the lightweight plastic cracked in the cold and they just couldn't stand up with heavy day-to-day use. After going through several of these I knew it was time to upgrade. I admired Gordon's magnificent *akhio* freight sled that he'd had custom made by an outfit in Anchorage. The heavy-duty molded plastic could take all kinds of abuse. And the sled could hold a massive load of firewood, water, and groceries. (Years later several friends and I would use that very same sled to carry Gordon's body down the mountainside from his cabin on Turnagain Arm.) But Gordon was a mountain of a man who could haul more freight than I could. So I bought a similar sled, but about half the size.

That wasn't the only time I followed Gordon's lead on sleds.

Tuesday night was orchestra rehearsal. Usually by the time Gordon and I would get back out to the woods it would be 10:30 or so. One winter night when we arrived at the trailhead and parked our vehicles, Gordon opened the trunk of his huge old Volvo and pulled out two shiny new Flexible Flyer sleds.

"Let's go!" he said. And we did.

We carried the sleds to the top of the hill. This gravel lane was our driveway from the main road down to our parking area. So it had two well-worn ruts, and the snow was packed hard, giving us our very own backwoods luge run. Gordon took one lane, and I took the other. And we did in fact fly flexibly down the hill, hollering all the way. As soon as we got to the bottom, we brushed ourselves off, picked up the sleds, and started back up again.

This went on for quite some time. On each ride down the hill I found myself spontaneously emitting a long descending glissando trill—something like a cross between a yodel and the haunted call of a boreal owl. The sky was clear. The moon was bright. And the air wasn't too cold. It was well after midnight when I got back to my cabin, where I grabbed my music notebook and promptly wrote down my "Boreal Sledding Call."

In his diet, Gordon was omnivorous. But he was very particular about the accoutrements of his daily life. If he found something he liked—whether it was Glenmorangie whisky, Alaskan Amber beer, the black size-XXL L.L.Bean T-shirts with the pockets in the front, or those special Portuguese orangewood toothpicks—he would stock up on that item. Sometime after our night of sledding we were at Gordon's cabin for a sauna. He pulled out a case of fancy stick matches he had just purchased: Rosebud brand. He gave me a box.

"Rosebud," of course, is the last dying word of Charles Foster Kane in Orson Welles's classic film *Citizen Kane*. It's the central mystery of the movie. But as we discover amid the rising flames of the final scene, Rosebud is the name of the sled from Kane's happiest childhood memory. Those two Flexible Flyers still hang on the backside of Gordon's cabin. And I still have that Rosebud matchbox.

Among the many benefits of life in the forest were the impromptu music lessons.

Early one Sunday, Gordon dropped by my cabin. I wasn't a morning person and Gordon was surprised to find me already sitting at my desk, looking very intent.

"What are you working on?" he asked.

"Oh. It's a piece for flute choir." I sighed. "It kept me up most of the night."

"What seems to be the problem?"

Over a hot cup of Postum (which I drank in lieu of coffee in those days), I showed Gordon the sequence of chords I had sketched out.

"I like the sound of these," I complained. "I just can't figure out what to *do* with them."

Gordon took a sip and gazed slowly around the room. Finally, his eyes settled on my refrigerator, which was covered in bright blue paisley wallpaper. After a long, pensive silence he said:

"Your chords are nice . . . But flutes like lots of notes and squiggles and curlicues . . . Just write your refrigerator!"

That's exactly what I did. I knew how to extract melodic lines from poetry, and how to translate them from birdsongs. But Gordon's observation put me on the path to discovering new ways that my music could sing.

I remember another afternoon sitting at the big desk in Gordon's cabin ("Command Central," as he called it), showing him the new piece I was working on. The tempo was slow and the textures were sparse, with lots of long sustained tones and glacially deliberate glissandi.

Gordon mused for a while. "Hmmm . . ." he muttered. "Things take time in the Arctic!"

A few years later, we were at Command Central again, looking over the draft of a new score I was composing for the Fairbanks Symphony. Gordon said nothing at all about the notes. He zeroed right in on the orchestration.

"You might want to add a flute here, doubling the first violins.

"And have you thought about pizzicato cellos here?"

I had studied orchestration in school. I had practiced orchestration in my own music. I had even taught orchestration at the University of Alaska. But Gordon's approach was organic—like a painter mixing colors, or a chef in the kitchen adding a pinch of this or a dash of that, here and there. This was the moment when I truly "got" orchestration.

But beyond little lessons like these, beyond introducing me to great music that I might not have sought out, beyond giving me commissions, premieres, and an orchestra to learn with, Gordon's greatest musical gift to me was his faith. Over the years Gordon often said to me: "I haven't always understood your music. But I've always believed in you."

What more could a young composer ask for?

Gordon wasn't my only musical advisor close at hand. In 1985, at a festival in Los Angeles, I'd been privileged to spend a few days in the company of one of my musical heroes, Morton Feldman. The following year Feldman died suddenly, and much too young. In his honor I composed *The Far Country of Sleep* (borrowing the title from the last line of a poem by John Haines about the death of his father). The Arctic Chamber Orchestra premiered the piece on a tour of Southeast Alaska. In a reversal of our usual roles, Gordon played percussion, and I conducted.

After the performance in Fairbanks, Leif Thompson said to me: "I really liked it . . . especially the middle. You know, the part where *nothing happens*. That's what you really want to do, isn't it?"

Leif's prophecy was prescient. But it would take me years to live up to it. Although I achieved it in a small ensemble with *The Light That Fills the World* (2001), it wasn't until *Dark Waves* (2007), *Become Ocean* (2012), and *Become Desert* (2017) that I learned how to sustain a single musical texture for an entire large-scale work. I needed time to develop the compositional technique to do this. But I also needed more experience out on the land.

Once Leif and I were camped on the Arctic coastal plain. In the evening light we saw a strange outcropping—a white monolith protruding from the tundra an indeterminate distance away. At first, we thought it might be a polar bear. But it never moved. So we set off in that direction. We walked and walked, yet we never seemed to get any closer to the white object. Then, suddenly, it rose up on sprawling wings and flew away—a snowy owl.

Another time Dennis Keeley and I were hiking on the coastal plain. As Dennis strode out ahead of me, I watched his feet rising and falling at a steady pace. But he looked as if he were walking in place, not moving forward at all. Immersed in that expanse with no trees and no prominent landmarks, we lose our sense of scale and distance—floating in undifferentiated space, suspended in time. *This* was what I was searching for in music.

For several years, as composer in residence with the Fairbanks Symphony, I presented an annual festival of new music called "American Originals." In 1988 our guest composer was Lou Harrison. Over the years Lou had taught me many lessons about the art of composition and the life of a composer. That week he also gave me the best conducting lesson I ever had. On the final program of the week was Lou's *Suite for Violin, Piano and Small Orchestra*, which I conducted. As a percussionist I'd always had steady time. And as an occasional conductor I'd always prided myself on my precision and attention to detail. After the dress rehearsal I asked Lou what he thought.

"You remind me of John Cage," he said.

Intrigued and vaguely flattered, I asked: "How so?"

"Well, you're more kinesthetic than John . . ."

I grew more flattered and more intrigued.

"When John used to conduct, he wanted to hear every detail of the music and he tried to show every nuance of the score. So, of course, the tempo would gradually slow down." Instantly I recognized that I was doing the very same thing. At the next evening's concert my conducting was leaner, crisper, and steadier in tempo—a style I've tried to maintain ever since.

This lesson from Lou was not just about conducting. It was also a lesson about teaching. Lou was fond of recalling that his teacher Henry Cowell would often begin a sentence by saying "As you know . . ." and then impart some wonderfully unexpected pearl of wisdom. In his own teaching Lou employed this technique brilliantly, using the gentle touch of flattery to prepare receptive minds for the gifts of learning.

For their concert in Alaska, Lou and his partner Bill Colvig brought with them the Sundanese *gamelan degung* Sekar Kembar. As far as we could determine, this was the first time a gamelan had been heard "live" in Alaska. Bill played various instruments in the ensemble and he was featured as a soloist playing the suling flute in Lou's tunefully sunny *Main Bersama-Sama* for horn, suling, and gamelan.

This was Lou's one and only visit to Alaska. But it was a homecoming for Bill. In the late 1930s Bill had left Berkeley to live for several years on the rough-and-ready frontier of Alaska and the Yukon, and he was excited to be back in the north again. After the concert Lou and Bill came out to my cabin for a party. The temperature in the forest that night was well into the 40s below zero. Accustomed to warmer climes, Lou was good-humored in his forbearance. Bill was in his element. The colder it got, the better he liked it.

I spent the better part of a decade living in my Walden, twice as long as I'd lived anyplace before. For most of my thirties I really believed that I could have it all and do it all. I led a physically demanding life in the woods, while I was still working a day job and playing in the orchestra. At the same time, Cindy and I were trying to sustain a serious long-term relationship without living together. I composed *A Northern Suite, Forest Without Leaves,* and *Strange Birds Passing* (the refrigerator flute choir piece) in that cabin in the bog. There I also composed *Coyote Builds North America* (a music theater work that was my first of several collaborations with Barry Lopez) and *The Far Country of Sleep.* Even so, I wasn't as productive as I wanted to be.

My music was suffering. My health was suffering. My relationship was suffering. Inevitably, something had to give.

Like Thoreau's cabin, my cabin wasn't far from town. And like Thoreau, I also had the company and counsel of two older friends and colleagues. If Gordon Wright was my Emerson, then John Haines was my Bronson Alcott. Or maybe it was the other way around. Either way, the intellectual stimulation and artistic encouragement that I got from John and Gordon created a space in which I could dream outsized dreams. We were living well off the map of mainstream culture. Yet there was always the sense that in this remote place we could make art that would stand shoulder-to-shoulder with art anywhere. I wouldn't advise any young artist to do what I did. Instead I'd say: Find your own private Walden, in the woods or in the city, whatever and wherever it may be. Make your own bad choices. And make them with conviction.

For a long time afterward, I viewed my years in the woods as my "lost decade." Yet if I had it to do over again, I'd probably make exactly the same mistakes. As difficult as that period was in some respects, it endures in my memory as a kind of dreamtime. This didn't come cheaply, for me or for people I love. It almost cost me the love of my life. But those years in the woods were essential for me, as an artist and as a man. In our shared solitude, I found a sense of community that I doubt I could've found in any other place. And the visions of music and of the world that emerged in that cabin have sustained me ever since.

| III |

The End of Winter

In the winters that I lived alone in the woods, the deeper the cold and the darkness got, the better I liked it. Or so I told myself.

In March 1989, an extreme cold front (an "omega block") settled over Alaska for three weeks. During one especially brutal week, the official high temperature in Fairbanks was never more than 40 degrees below zero. At my cabin, in one of the notoriously cold low-lying areas around town, it didn't rise above 55 below.

Alaska's record-low temperature (set on my birthday, January 23, in 1971) was 80 below zero. One night during the omega block, the National Weather Service predicted that this mark would be surpassed. Although that didn't happen, the thermometer at my cabin registered 78 below. A couple of nights later, the barometric pressure at Northway (near Alaska's border with the Yukon) was 31.85 inches of mercury—the highest reading ever recorded in North America. At temperatures like these, one false move can be costly. When a neighbor back in the woods beyond me couldn't get his propane stove to work, he brought the tank inside his cabin to warm it up. The tank exploded. Badly burned, my neighbor dragged himself through the night, almost two miles out to the road. I still remember the drops of frozen blood all along the trail.

As the cold deepened, Fairbanks was smothered under a dense blanket of frozen smog. The wisest course of action was to hunker down and wait it out. In the middle of all this, Cindy told me that after ten years together she wasn't sure she saw a future for our relationship. This shouldn't have come as a surprise to me, but it did. I was shattered. Gordon had recently moved to his cabin in the mountains south of Anchorage. So there I was—heartsick, a little frightened by the fierce cold, and feeling utterly alone. Suddenly, my isolation no longer seemed so splendid. It was more like solitary confinement.

I had no idea when or how I would come out of this dark place. And then came the worst environmental disaster in Alaska's history. On March 24, 1989, the *Exxon Valdez* ran aground on Bligh Reef, spilling thirty million gallons or more of crude oil into the icy waters of Prince William Sound. That oil, originally extracted at Prudhoe Bay and transported eight hundred miles through the Trans-Alaska Pipeline, eventually covered thirteen hundred miles of coastline and eleven thousand square miles of ocean.

My girlfriend was gone. My best friend was gone. I was alone in the forest. And now the doomsday scenario we had all feared had struck this place that we loved so deeply. It felt like my life in Alaska might be over. But I couldn't imagine who I might be without Alaska. As an Alaskan, I felt special. This feeling came from living close to the earth, surrounded by wild country, far from the urban centers of North America. It came from living among a relatively sparse human population, with wild animals as our neighbors. It came from my friendships with Alaska Native people, and from my experiences in villages where people have lived for countless centuries by the wisdom of the earth. It also came from the cold. The fierce, hard, clear winter cold of the northern interior felt as immutable as the peaks of the Alaska Range towering in the distance, across the Tanana Flats. I couldn't have imagined how quickly and dramatically that would change.

A decade later, on New Year's Eve in 1999, Cindy (now my wife) and I hosted a bonfire at our house in the hills north of Fairbanks. As the twenty-first century dawned in Alaska, our thermometer read 57 degrees below zero. We, and our friends, reveled in it. But the following winter the temperature in Fairbanks never reached 40 below. This was a first, in the brief recorded history of local weather. However, it would quickly become the new normal. High-temperature records began to be set with regularity, in both summer and winter. I remember the first time that we saw lightning and heard thunder in December, which was followed by a heavy freezing rain. It had always been that the roads around town were better in winter, when a hard crust of dry, compacted snow filled in all the potholes and offered plenty of traction. Now we had frequent freezing and thawing, and treacherous glazes of thick black ice.

One spring afternoon, while watching birds at a bog near our house, I was startled to hear the unmistakable call—*congare-e-e-up*—of a red-winged blackbird. This is a bird that I'd first come to know in Okefenokee Swamp, thousands of miles to the south, in Georgia. It was certainly not a resident species of interior Alaska. Yet here it was. And ever since then the redwings have appeared each spring, in that same northern bog. Over the next decade, we saw the climate of Alaska continue to warm at an alarming rate. In a very real way, the Alaska that we knew was beginning to disappear.

Meanwhile, the wildfire season increased in length and intensity. In 2004, it lasted all summer. From June through September, temperatures soared, and there was almost no precipitation. That summer, 6.3 million acres in Alaska—an area larger than the state of Vermont—went up in flames. In northern Alaska, summer is the season of endless daylight, and yet, day after day, we didn't see the sun. The smell of smoke was omnipresent, and the air was dangerously polluted. The public was warned to limit exertion and to stay indoors as much as possible. The Red Cross set up smoke-respite centers to provide people with sanctuary from the oppressive conditions. Many fled south, in search of cleaner air. In its magnitude and intensity, that fire season dramatically surpassed all those previously recorded. But subsequent summers have come all too close to matching it.

In a nation addicted to petroleum, Alaska is a colony of Big Oil. Back in the 1980s and '90s, as oil money overflowed the coffers of the State of Alaska, new freeways were built around Fairbanks. Shopping malls and ranch-style houses sprouted like mushrooms. On a visit to Seattle in the 2000s, driving on the freeway, I turned to Cindy and asked, rhetorically, "Since when did Seattle become Los Angeles?" On our return north, we stopped for a couple of days in Anchorage, and I found myself asking, "So when did Anchorage become Seattle?" And when we got back home, I couldn't help but quip, "And when did Fairbanks become Anchorage?"

Like those more southerly cities, Fairbanks is built for the automobile. And perhaps nowhere in the world is the Southern California model of suburban living more glaringly inappropriate. Like Los Angeles, Fairbanks is situated in a natural inversion basin, in which a broken ring of hills traps colder, heavier air close to the ground. For decades now, the air in Fairbanks has been more polluted than the air in L.A. In winter, ice fog is a naturally occurring phenomenon along the Chena and Tanana Rivers. But mixed with automobile exhaust and woodsmoke from residential heating, it becomes a toxic pall of frozen smog.

Public transportation in Fairbanks is woefully inadequate. Despite the tireless attempts of motivated citizens, there is still no significant recycling of solid waste. There's also virtually no renewable energy. Almost everyone heats with oil or wood. Electricity is almost exclusively generated from fossil fuels. As a result, residents of the Golden Heart City must have among the largest carbon footprints of any people who have ever lived. At the same time, climate change has become an undeniable fact of day-to-day life here.

Farther north, the changes have been even more alarming, as a phenomenon called Arctic acceleration has taken effect. Global warming is occurring twice as fast in the Arctic as in other regions of the earth. For me, this is personal. I love Alaska with a passion that is almost erotic. I first stood on the shore of the Arctic Ocean in 1979. During the following thirty years, the thickness of the circumpolar ice decreased by 50 percent. By the middle of the current century there will almost certainly be no more multi-year pack ice.

Looking at satellite images of the retreat of the sea ice is like looking at photos of someone I love wasting away from a horrible disease. It is heartbreaking. For me, as for so many others, Alaska had been the geography of hope—the last great untouched place in North America. But now, in a few short decades, it's become one of the most threatened parts of this increasingly threatened earth. Some may see promising opportunities for wealth in an ice-free Arctic. But, as the ice disappears and the waters rise, what will take the Arctic's place in the human imagination?

A friend of mine once observed that a piece like *In the White Silence* might one day come to be a kind of archaeological artifact of the Alaska that we knew and loved. Maybe so. Yet I want my music to be more than an elegy for what we have lost, more than a lamentation for a world that is melting. Music is my way of imagining how the world is, and how it might be, with or without us.

Long before Europeans came to northwest Alaska, Maniilaq—the Iñupiaq prophet of the Kobuk River—predicted that there would come a time when a season would occur twice in succession. Ever since then, most people have believed that this prophecy would come to pass as two consecutive winters. But Maniilaq did not say. And today it seems more likely to come as two successive summers.

What will Alaska be after the end of winter? I will not be there to find out. I only pray that there will still be people in Alaska, and that, like the First Alaskans, they will live far more lightly on the earth than we have.

Out of the Woods

I left the woods for as good a reason as I went there . . . It seemed to me that I had several more lives to live, and could not spare any more time for that one.

—HENRY DAVID THOREAU

As the dark and lonely winter of 1988–89 drew to a close, I felt a growing urge to escape, to lose myself in something larger than my own pain and sense of loss. If I was lost, then I wanted to be completely lost.

My friend the bush pilot Dennis Miller agreed to fly me out to the Yukon River. He dropped me off at the confluence of the Tanana and the Yukon, near the village of Tanana. I made my camp, and waited.

I'd already been waiting for weeks, filled with feelings of absence, longing, and anticipation. Now the whole world around me seemed to amplify and resonate with those feelings. For the next few days I sat and walked along the riverbank—listening, waiting, trying to imagine the force of two thousand miles of ice three feet thick breaking free and beginning to flow at five miles per hour. There in the overpowering presence of the great river, my personal troubles began to seem small and insignificant.

The glassy tones of candle ice swirling in whirlpools, the intricate arpeggios of meltwater dripping, and the ominous rumbling and grinding of icebergs resonated deep in my dreams. And when the ice finally broke free, something inside me broke with it. I felt released.

I returned to Fairbanks, feeling that no matter how things turned out with Cindy, my life in Alaska would continue.

In early June, Wilbur Mills and I flew up to the Arctic Refuge and made a base camp on the banks of the Jago River, near its headwaters in the northern foothills of the Brooks Range. We were pushing the season, and soon found ourselves trapped in our small tent while a spring blizzard howled. During three days of icy wind and heavy, driving snow we hardly left our sleeping bags. In the cold air and flat gray light, the line between waking and dreaming became blurred. I was haunted by recurring visions of a large brown bear, stalking me across the open tundra.

Near midnight on the third day, the weather broke and we emerged. Before the storm, the river had been raging with spring meltwater. Now it had frozen to a trickle. We walked across to the other side and began climbing. Halfway up the slope we came upon a small basin full of grass tussocks, covered with new snow and bathed in warm golden light. Wilbur set up his tripod and began to work.

I continued on, hiking to the crest of the ridge, where I hoped to look out across the coastal plain and catch a glimpse of the Arctic Ocean. At last I reached the ridgeline and a large stone outcrop. Carefully placing my steps over the wet, snowy rocks, I climbed to the top. The view beyond was more breathtaking than I had imagined—the vast coastal plain sweeping east and west to the horizon, and fifty miles north to the shore of the Beaufort Sea, where the midnight sun hung suspended between a brooding, leaden sky and the luminous pack ice. I stood transfixed.

Suddenly I was seized by a vivid sense that I was not alone. I felt the palpable presence of another. The hair stood up on the back of my neck. Then it passed.

I don't know how long I stood there frozen in the beauty of the place and the moment. Eventually I bowed, turned, and began to climb slowly down the rocks, back the way I had come. Near the bottom of the outcrop I stopped. There, crossing my boot prints in the snow, were the fresh tracks of a large grizzly bear. While I'd been standing no more than thirty feet above, the bear had crossed my path. His trail descended in a broad arc, disappearing down toward the river.

That night I slept without dreaming. The next afternoon I saw him.

We were sitting in camp when he appeared on a gravel bar a couple of hundred yards upstream. Wilbur grabbed his camera and we moved cautiously in the bear's direction. At what we judged to be a safe distance, we sat down in the bushes and Wilbur began photographing.

The bear was a strapping young male, ripping willows up by the roots, hunting for ground squirrels. It was early in the season and it probably hadn't been long since he'd emerged from hibernation. Even so, the bear looked very healthy, his coat shiny. We watched in awe as he made his way through the thicket, churning up the tundra vegetation like a bulldozer.

Gradually the bear moved in our direction, and we retreated back to camp. He kept coming our way. When he emerged from the willows just above our tent, Wilbur and I started talking to him.

"Hey, brother bear. Great country you have here. We're just passing through. We won't stay long."

He walked on toward us.

"Hey, now. We don't want any trouble. There's plenty of room out here for all of us."

Wilbur kept photographing. I picked up the borrowed rifle we had with us.

The bear kept coming.

We had no place to go. The river was at our backs, and there were no trees to climb.

About thirty feet away from us, the bear stopped. He sat up on his hind legs and sniffed the air. He dropped back down on all fours and walked in a tight circle.

I raised the rifle to my shoulder. But I was trembling so hard that even if I'd been able to bring myself to pull the trigger, I might have missed. Besides, the .30-30 was too small for the job, and an angry wounded bear would've been a worst-case scenario. I lowered the gun.

The bear sat up again. He snapped his jaws, growled, and made a short bluff charge in our direction. I gasped for breath, Wilbur put his camera down, and we edged back toward the river. As we did, a strong gust of wind rose up, carrying our scent directly to the bear.

He turned and galloped off across the tundra. We watched until he disappeared over a high ridge.

At the end of June, Cindy and our friend Debbie Miller (Dennis's wife) decided to take their kids up to the Refuge for a base camp on the Okpilak River ("The River with No Willows"). I'd been commissioned to create a radio piece about the Arctic. So my pal Leif and I arranged to fly into Cindy and Debbie's camp, to spend a couple of days before taking off on a backpack trip to record sounds.

As I unloaded my pack from the plane Cindy smiled sweetly and asked me in her most offhand tone: "So . . . You wanna get married?"

Mustering all the nonchalance I could, I replied, "Sure."

Dennis was in the Refuge, flying surveys of the Porcupine caribou herd. (The Arctic coastal plain is the calving ground of the herd, which that year numbered 178,000 animals.) A few days later he dropped in, landing his Super Cub on the tundra, to present us with a wedding cake and a couple of bottles of champagne imported from Fairbanks, four hundred roadless miles to the south.

We hiked across a small creek, over the tundra, and up a hill at the north end of the valley, where Cindy and I exchanged our vows. These were the endless days of the Arctic summer. The sun was low in the north and everything was bathed in deep golden evening light. No one had a watch. So we'll never know whether we were married on June 30 or July 1.

We strolled back down to camp, where we ate wedding cake, drank champagne, and danced around a fire we built on a gravel bar in the river. The sun disappeared behind the ridge. We put the kids to bed, returned to the fire, and began telling stories. Suddenly something caught my ear. I ran up the riverbank to get away from the sound of the water. Cindy, Leif, and Debbie followed. There, on the very spot where we had spoken our vows, sat a lone wolf, howling to the sky. Above the wolf, a pair of snowy owls circled on the cool air.

Back in Fairbanks, I moved out of the woods and up onto the hillside with Cindy and Sage, who was now moving into his teen years. I was still working at the public radio station, but I wasn't happy in the job and at thirty-six I'd begun to feel it was now or never to devote myself to composing full-time. I had no idea how I'd make ends meet without a regular paycheck. My boss offered me the opportunity to continue working on a half-time basis. So I did what I often did in situations like these. I called my friend and mentor Lou Harrison. As usual, Lou went right to the heart of the matter: "There are no half-time jobs, John Luther. Only half-time salaries."

I promptly quit my job and never looked back. Cindy enthusiastically endorsed my decision. She told me not to worry. She had a good-paying full-time job with the Fairbanks North Star Borough, and she could cover for us if need be. Then, just a few months later, Cindy decided that she'd had enough, too. She quit the Borough and started her own business, helping nonprofit organizations in Alaska find money to do their good work. (Several years later, that business would expand to become national and eventually international in its reach.)

Neither of us had any supplemental income. We lived cheaply, at first renting our house and my studio for relative pittances, until eventually we could afford to buy them. Cindy's office was a funky little cabin down the hill from the studio. (We called it "the Hovel.") We had no car payments. We shared a battered 1987 Mazda that I dubbed "Alice." I would coax that old rattletrap down the road, exhorting: "To the moon, Alice! To the moon!" And when they finally hauled her away to the junkyard, the odometer read more than 237,000 miles—just shy of a one-way trip to the moon. Fairbanks is hardly a culinary capital, and fortunately, Cindy is a wonderful cook, so it wasn't much of a hardship that we didn't eat out very often. The sartorial emphasis in Alaska is always on function before fashion, so we didn't need to wear fancy clothes. We didn't have much furniture, or a lot of other possessions. For the next two decades this was how we got by. Somehow, we even managed to get Sage through college.

The little house that we shared was smaller than the cabin I'd lived in alone. Sage had the only bedroom, down in the basement. Cindy and I slept in the loft above the living room. The ceiling up there was so low that I couldn't even stand upright. There was no room in the house for me to work. At first, I kept my cabin in the spruce bog as my studio. But running back and forth took too much of my time. So when Cindy and our friend Glynn found a small cabin hidden in the birch-and-aspen forest nearby, I sold my old cabin to my neighbors Frank and Nora Foster.

For the next twenty-odd years, this new cabin would be my studio. There I began work on *Earth and the Great Weather*, subtitled "A Sonic Geography of the Arctic." *Earth* is a celebration of the physical geography of the Arctic National Wildlife Refuge, the homeland of both the Iñupiat (Inuit) and Gwich'in (Athabascan) peoples. The conceptual ground of the piece is a series of "Arctic Litanies"—found poems composed from indigenous names for places, plants, birds, and the seasons. Spoken and sung in the Gwich'in and Iñupiat languages, these words seemed to me to come directly out of the earth itself, resonating deeply with centuries of experience living in that country, evoking an authentic poetry of place.

The musical and narrative arc of the piece grew from a single name. Naalagiagvik ("The Place Where You Go to Listen") is a place on the coast of the Arctic Ocean, named by a woman for whom it had special power. There, when she sat alone, she could hear the voices of her ancestors and understand the languages of the birds. From that place, I imagined this woman traveling alone, crossing the great plain into the mountains of the Brooks Range, over the Arctic Divide and on into the vast forest of the south slope. Moving east through the home country of the Gwich'in people, she eventually makes her way back through the mountains and out to the coast at Pataktuk ("Where the Waves Splash, Hitting Again and Again").

Even as I worked on the radio piece, I came to realize that I'd embarked on something much larger. And three years later, in the winter of 1993, my ensemble—including the Gwich'in performers Adeline Peter Raboff and Lincoln Tritt, and the Iñupiat performers Doreen Simmonds and James Nageak—premiered an evening-length version of *Earth and the Great*

Weather, commissioned to celebrate the tenth anniversary of the Festival of Alaska Native Arts.

We were rehearsing *One That Stays All Winter*, the litany of birds. In the middle of the piece Lincoln intoned an especially resonant name in his Gwich'in dialect:

". . . *Aahaalak* . . ."

A few seconds later, James echoed: "*Aaqhaaliq.*"

Everybody stopped.

James looked at Lincoln. "You said '*Aaqhaaliq.*'"

Lincoln looked at James. "*You* said '*Aahaalak.*'"

As it turns out, the name for the long-tailed duck is the same in both Iñupiaq and Gwichi'in. The call of the duck is onomatopoeic. The bird sings its own name.

From then on, James and Lincoln always greeted each other with a hearty call of "*A-haa-lik!*"

During my vigil on the banks of the Yukon River, waiting for the ice to break up, an idea had come to me. I imagined music invoking elemental violence in nature—howling storms, raging wildfires, and glaciers calving into the sea—violence at once terrifying and comforting, transpersonal and purifying. In that spirit I began work on *Strange and Sacred Noise* (1991–97), a concert-length cycle of pieces for percussion quartet.

I'd been reading books about chaos theory and fractals— those deeply symmetrical forms arising from the reiteration of simple processes, forms that we recognize in coastlines, mountain ranges, snowflakes, and lightning bolts. This inspired me to imagine a kind of "sonic geometry"—fractal forms made audible.

I started with the Cantor set—a simple, self-similar form that begins with a line segment. From that segment, the middle third is removed, leaving two segments. From each of these, the middle third is removed . . . and so on to infinity, dissolving into "*a strange dust of points, arranged in clusters, infinitely many yet infinitely sparse.*" Originally regarded as little more than a mathematical curiosity, the Cantor set was discovered in the early twentieth century to be a remarkable model of the self-similar nature of intermittent noise in electrical transmissions. Electrical transmissions contain within them periods of steady signal alternating with bursts of noise. Within this noise are minute periods of silence. The patterns of these signal/noise/silence cycles appear to remain constant, no matter how long or brief a period of time is sampled.

I wanted to simulate this form in musical time. The result was . . . *dust into dust* . . . for two snare drums and two field drums. Insistent, accented figures are interrupted by periods of steady, pianissimo drum rolls. Yet the apparently continuous sound of a drum roll is also intermittent, containing within it (at the microtemporal level) countless minute gaps of silence. Over the course of nine minutes or so, the accented figures gradually dissolve into quiet dust (rolls), and then into silence, gradually expanding again into dust, and explosive noise.

For other sections of *Strange and Sacred Noise*, I devised my own homemade fractals. The piece titled *solitary and time-breaking waves* is scored for four tam-tams (untuned gongs). I puzzled for weeks over a musical form that could contain the roaring tam-tams without constraining them. On a flight from Fairbanks to Anchorage, gazing out the window at Denali and Mount Foraker, it finally came to me. I pulled the notebook out of my pocket and drew four layers of waveforms, rising and falling. The top layer had seven waves. The next layer down had five. The next layer had three waves. And the bottom layer was a single large wave. Underneath the drawing I wrote: "This is it!"

As simple as it was, I knew that I'd arrived at something

powerful. I decided to employ variations on that form in other sections of *Strange and Sacred Noise*. And in subsequent years, I've used those same 1/3/5/7 waves again and again, in pieces from *Red Arc/Blue Veil* to *Become Ocean*. I've always been a formalist. I want my music to be arrestingly physical. But even when we're not consciously aware of it, formal structure—the mathematics and geometry of composition—gives the music a deeper coherence, a feeling of objectivity and inevitability.

Another "classical" fractal that intrigued me was the Sierpiński gasket—an Eiffel Tower of reiterated nesting triangles. I translated this form into a piece for eight timpani (two drums for each player) playing continuous rolls in rising and falling lines, and sent the score via fax to my collaborators. A few days later, the phone rang. The voice on the other end was unmistakable.

"John . . ." he began.

"Al . . ." I replied.

"It's a piece of *shit!*"

Allen Otte is not known for mincing words. And I knew he was right. The piece just didn't work with timpani. It was awkward to play, and it didn't resonate. Clearly, it was time for me to go for broke. A week or so later I sent the final version off to Al: *triadic iteration lattices*—for four air-raid sirens.

After going back and forth this way for more than five years, in April 1997 Percussion Group Cincinnati premiered the full version of *Strange and Sacred Noise*. During our rehearsal of the siren piece, the lights in the theater started flashing. Alarms began buzzing loudly and a robot voice burst over the loudspeaker instructing everyone to evacuate the building. Dutifully, we drifted outside with everyone else and stood around, sipping coffee and doing our best to look nonchalant until the "all-clear" was given.

In the summer of 2000, my ensemble traveled to London, to present *Earth and the Great Weather* at the Almeida Opera festival. In previous productions of *Earth*, I'd played percussion and conducted. But we had an all-star ensemble, so I sat in the balcony, taking it all in.

Things were going very well. The first of the three big percussion pieces—*Drums of Winter*—was unusually strong. As it ended, I noticed a fidgety figure a little farther down the balcony. Even in the dark theater, his discomfort was apparent in his body language. The performance continued. As the group Synergy Vocals began singing the new parts I'd composed for this production, I forgot all about the fellow down below. The quiet *Arctic Litanies*—with singers, strings, and spoken voices—floated beautifully through the space.

Then the drums returned, with *Deep and Distant Thunder.* For the next twelve or thirteen minutes the drummers pounded out driving cross-rhythms inspired by Alaska Native dance music. They swung into the final unison passage with fearsome energy and precision, nailing the last explosive cadence to the brick walls of the theater.

There was a collective sigh from the audience. And as the delicate tinkling of candle ice began to emerge, an angry voice rang out, shattering the stillness:

"Too LOUD!!!" followed in a stage mutter by: "*. . . and fucking unpleasant, as well . . .*"

I didn't have to look to know who it was.

The show went on. It kept getting better, and once again I forgot about my unhappy neighbor in the balcony. When the drummers returned for their final number, they launched into the opening unison with startling ferocity. Mr. Unpleasant leaped to his feet, threw his hands into the air, and stormed out, snorting. This only encouraged the drummers, who played on with almost frightening energy.

Several years later, Cindy and I had the pleasure of dining with the legendary percussionist Jan Williams and his wife. Jan had been close friends with Morton Feldman, and he's well known for his performances of Feldman's music, including *The King of Denmark*—an exquisitely delicate solo work that hovers throughout on the threshold of audibility.

During his years teaching at SUNY Buffalo, Jan had led several performances of my music, including the drum quartets from *Earth and the Great Weather*, so I told him the story from London. Jan laughed, and without missing a beat he picked up the thread:

"Yeah. I know that guy . . . Or maybe it was his brother . . ."

"Really?" I credulously replied.

"Yeah." Then Jan told his story:

"I was giving a concert in London, and I was playing *The King*. It was going really well, and I was moving into the final couple of minutes. All of a sudden, this guy calls out from the back of the hall:

"We kahnt HEEE-ah yooooooooou!!!"

Too soft? Too loud? Apparently for some listeners only a narrow range of dynamics is acceptable in music. But although I don't believe that poor fellow at the Almeida Theatre was right about the drums being too loud (and I'm hardly a credible witness as to their unpleasantness), he may have had a point in theory. Music *can* be too large for the space in which it's performed. Sometimes intentionally so . . .

Strange and Sacred Noise intentionally pushes the limits. It bounces off the walls, saturating the acoustic space, and the psycho-acoustic space of our perceptions. It buzzes the eardrums, rattles the rib cage, and overwhelms our senses. In response to the complex, high-energy sounds—thundering drums, roaring tam-tams, clanging bells, wailing sirens—our ears play tricks on us. We hear things that aren't really there.

The strange power of noise can open doorways to the ecstatic. Musical traditions throughout the world have explored this power for centuries. I knew it from my years as a rock drummer. But my most profound experiences of this have come through the all-night drumming, chanting, and dancing of the Iñupiat and Yup'ik peoples. The rapid reiteration of loud, acoustically complex sounds alters our consciousness. In this state, as my Native friends might say, we can travel to and from the spirit world.

One winter morning I boarded a jet in Fairbanks at 45 below and flew north—across the Yukon River, the Brooks Range, and the Arctic coastal plain—to Utkiagvik (Barrow), where it was a balmy 33 below (although with the wind chill it was closer to 80 below). I'd come for Kivgiq, the Messenger Feast—three nights of traditional Iñupiaq drumming, singing, and dancing. Groups from all the Iñupiat villages in Alaska and four villages in Arctic Canada had come to the northernmost point in Alaska for this midwinter festival of feasting, gift giving, and celebration.

By this time, I knew a few Iñupiaq songs, at least roughly. Their angular melodic contours, asymmetrical rhythms, powerful unison choruses, and deep, explosive drums had become integral parts of the soundscape of my life. The rhythmic foundation of 2 + 3 or 2 + 2 + 3 had been my point of departure for the three drum quartets in *Earth and the Great Weather*. Sometimes called the Iñupiaq "heartbeat," this asymmetrical pulse is both more sophisticated and more energizing than the steady 4/4 backbeat of rock 'n' roll. After a strong dance group from the Arctic coast, even the best rock bands sound rhythmically square.

Kivgiq is not held every year. It occurs after a prosperous hunting season, when there is enough material wealth to allow for widespread gift giving. At the heart of it is Kalukaq (the Box Drum Dance)—an elaborate ceremony grounded in the myth of Eagle Mother, who brought the gift of music and dancing to the People.

Before the dancers enter, two men bring out a tall extension ladder, which they prop against the rafters. One of them climbs the ladder and lowers a rope that's already been hung in place. A third man brings out the box drum and ties it to the rope, where it hangs, swinging freely. The drum is made of plywood, about one foot by one foot by three feet in dimension. It's painted bright blue and yellow. The top is finished with jagged edges (representing mountain peaks) and adorned with a single eagle feather.

The drummers, singers, and dancers enter, chanting in unison to the steady clicking of sticks on the rims of the drums. The box drummer sits on a chair facing the wooden drum, his back to the audience. He wears a headdress made from the head and wing feathers of a loon. Several young male dancers take their places sitting on the floor, facing him.

The ensemble of twelve frame drummers (all men) sits in a single, long row. The drummers are dressed in bright blue *qaspaqs*. Most of the women, in vibrant red, sit in three rows behind the drummers. But several younger women stand facing the box drummer, holding long wands tipped with feathers.

When everyone is in place, as the chant continues, the frame drummers begin playing full force, until the box drummer cuts them off with a wildly irregular beat. In silence, he begins an elaborate series of gestures. He bows forward from the waist, extending his right arm above his head, full length on the floor. The male dancers do the same and the young women extend their feathered wands.

The singers begin a new chant, accompanied by clicks on the

drum rims. Slowly, the box drummer pulls his arm backward. He holds it there for a moment, and then brings it forward rapidly, stopping just short of striking the drum. He does this many times, with stylized gestures of great formality. When he finally strikes the drum, in a sudden unison with the frame drums, the sound is stunning.

As the dance proceeds, the box drummer begins to swing the drum on its rope. As he swings left, the male dancers move to his right, like puppets on a string. He performs an elaborate series of movements with the drum, which the dancers mirror in reverse.

Several minutes into the dance another dancer appears, also wearing a loon headdress. With each drumbeat he hops two-footed, moving around the box drum. Gradually he closes the circle, moving closer and closer to the box drummer. Suddenly, in a marvelously fluid movement on his backswing, the box drummer hands the heavy mallet to the dancer, who becomes the new drummer. All this happens without missing a beat.

About 2:00 a.m. the festival ends with a processional of all the dance groups, and a few songs sung and danced by virtually everyone in the space. A hundred Iñupiat drummers playing in unison is a sound I'll never forget.

This drumming, chanting, and dancing encompasses what we usually call art. But this is not self-expression, or art for art's sake. Kivgiq is woven more deeply into the larger fabric of life—the life of the individual, the life of the community, the life of the land, and the life of the animals and the spirits that inhabit it. This is something that so many of us have lost in our lives. And although I'm a visitor in this culture, tonight I would rather be here in this high school gymnasium than in any symphony hall, opera house, or church I can imagine.

I've learned much from my Alaska Native friends and neighbors. But I've always been reluctant to incorporate Native music into my own. I have the greatest respect for the integrity of those traditions. And I try to draw my music directly from the earth, as unmediated as possible by culture—my own or anyone else's. I've borrowed directly from Native music only once (in my *Five Athabascan Dances* and *Five Yup'ik Dances*), with explicit permission from the songmakers and songkeepers. And on another occasion, I was able to return the gift.

My friend Adeline Peter Raboff asked me to compose songs on two poems she had written in her native Gwich'in dialect. Although I don't speak or understand Gwich'in, much of the text of *Earth and the Great Weather* is in the language, so I'd had it in my ears for some time. I asked Adeline to record herself speaking the poems. Listening carefully, I transcribed the melodies of her speech. Adeline used those two songs at a youth camp to help teach Athabascan children a little of their ancestral language.

The following winter she traveled out to Bethel, in Yup'ik (Bering Sea Inuit) country. While she was there, she sang one of the songs. A woman who heard her asked Adeline for permission to translate the text into Yup'ik and to sing the song at the Naming Ceremony for her daughter. Not long after that, Adeline was in Anaktuvuk Pass, where someone asked for permission to sing the song in the local dialect of the Nunamiut, the Inuit people of the Brooks Range. Since then, that little song has been shared with people in other villages throughout Alaska, and it's profoundly gratifying to me that it has traveled full circle.

For the fall of 1996, I was invited to teach at Bennington College in Vermont. This was the first time in decades that either Cindy or I had been outside of Alaska for an extended period. The timing was fortuitous. My mother had cancer, and she was in the final months of her life.

Between my parents' drinking and the protracted disintegration of their marriage, and our moving around from place to place, I'd had an unsettled childhood. I'd left home as soon as I could, and put as much distance as I could between my family and myself. When my father died, I hadn't seen him in several years. In its own way, my relationship with my mother was just as complex. But soon after Tom's death, Alice had made a special point of sitting me down and directly apologizing to me.

"I'm sorry," she said. "I know I wasn't a very good mother."

I admired her courage and honesty. That simple, generous act seemed to lift a heavy weight off both of us.

Cindy and I were back and forth between Vermont and Georgia several times that fall. And we were with Alice in her home, at her bedside, when she passed away.

We returned to Alaska in the depth of winter. Almost immediately I began composing *In the White Silence*. I wanted this to be the biggest, most beautiful thing I'd ever done. In part it would be a memorial for my mother. Beyond that, it would be a paean to the windswept expanses of the Arctic.

Several years earlier I'd composed *Dream in White on White*, for string quartet, harp, and string orchestra, using only the seven tones of Pythagorean diatonic tuning (the acoustically perfect intervals that are roughly approximated by the C-major scale of the piano). When I shared the score of that piece with Lou Harrison, he observed that I'd rediscovered the diatonic scale for myself, as "something wild, fresh, and new." Now, adding two vibraphones and celesta to the ensemble of *Dream*, I returned to that world of the "white notes" on a more expansive plane.

For the next two years I worked on *In the White Silence*, composing more than a thousand measures of music without a single sharp or flat. From time to time, I would put it down and resume work on the slowly evolving cycle of *Strange and Sacred Noise*.

Those two pieces were twins, born at the same time. Yet on the surface, they couldn't have been more different. *In the White Silence* is seventy-five minutes of continuous music without a single moment of actual silence. By contrast, the seventy minutes of *Strange and Sacred Noise* encompasses several minutes of composed silence.

Both noise and silence are invitations to listen more deeply to the world around us. John Cage observed that when we try to ignore noise, it disturbs us. Yet when we stop and actually *listen* to noise, we find it fascinating. As Cage's *4'33"* (his "silent piece") reminds us, there is no such thing as silence. There is always something to hear. And when we are listening, the whole world becomes music.

Cage is probably the best known of a lineage extending from Charles Ives, Henry Cowell, Ruth Crawford Seeger, Edgard Varèse, and Harry Partch to Peter Garland, Michael Byron, Lois V. Vierk, and other composers of my generation. In my lifetime I've been fortunate to know Cage, Morton Feldman, and Dane Rudhyar, and to enjoy close friendships with Lou Harrison, James Tenney, and Pauline Oliveros. This is my musical family. None of these composers sounds like any of the others. What they share in common is their independence from the orthodoxies of European classical music, and their commitment to the power of music as *sound*. Each in their own way started from scratch, to imagine and create their own unique musical world.

In the 1990s I began to travel more frequently—for teaching stints at Bennington and the Oberlin Conservatory, and for regular trips to New York. From Fairbanks, it's a long journey to pretty much anywhere. After September 11, 2001, as airport security changed radically, the indignities and discomforts of air travel grew. At the same time I became more and more concerned about the contribution of unnecessary travel to climate disruption, and increasingly protective of my time in the studio. But the deeper truth was that I just didn't feel comfortable being away from home. Several days before a trip I'd begin to feel anxious, and my anxiety would crescendo.

Sometime in the nineties, I was preparing to leave home when the phone rang. It was my friend Adeline calling to wish me a happy birthday. I hadn't seen her since she'd returned from an extended stay in Washington, D.C., where she was working on the campaign to keep oil drilling out of the Arctic National Wildlife Refuge.

"It's been too long," I said.

"We should get together," said Adeline.

"I'd like that. I'm leaving for New York tomorrow. Why don't I call you when I get back?"

"You could. But why don't I come up this afternoon?"

We set a time and I went back to the studio. A few hours later, as I walked up to the house, Adeline was just getting out of her car. I put on some tea, and we sat down to talk.

Adeline is a striking woman with sharp features, dark hair, and deep brown eyes. On her chin she wears a traditional Gwich'in three-pronged tattoo. Her voice is rich and clear. Her gaze is strong but gentle.

We talked a little about our work. We caught up on the goings-on in our lives. I said nothing about my anxiety. Then Adeline asked me: "Did I ever tell you the story of how my father passed away?"

"I don't think so," I said.

Adeline's father, Steven Peter, was a leader among his Gwich'in people, and a healer. When Steven would say, "Someone in the family will carry this on," Adeline always assumed he was talking about someone else. She imagined the gift would skip a generation.

At the end of his life Steven was hospitalized in Fairbanks. As his family gathered around, Adeline began to make arrangements for his last rites. But Steven told her that he wanted to die at Old

John Lake, upriver from Arctic Village, far from any roads. So Adeline chartered a flight, checked Steven out of the hospital, and flew north with her father and her mother, Katherine. In the village everyone turned out to say goodbye. Then father, mother, and daughter flew out to Old John Lake.

"The first thing we did was to build a shelter," said Adeline.

They made Steven comfortable and began the vigil. They prayed. They sang. They told stories. They sat in silence, keeping watch as Steven left his body.

"His hands died first," said Adeline. "Over the next two days, other parts of his body passed away, one by one. Finally, his spirit left.

"After he died, my mother walked back to Arctic Village alone. It took her two days."

Adeline paused, took a sip of her tea, and said: "I need to be getting back down the hill. But I'd like to say a prayer for you— the way my father used to . . ."

She asked me to sit in a chair in the center of the room. Standing behind me, Adeline pulled something out of her bag. I thought it might be a rattle. I closed my eyes, and slipped into another state of mind. I don't know how long I sat there. But when I opened my eyes I was calm as a stone basking in the sunlight.

The next morning, I took off on my journey feeling firmly rooted in my home.

In the fall of 1998, I taught at Oberlin. The students were a lively bunch. I loved their energy, and I admired their creativity. Most of them were as cocksure of themselves as I had been. And, as I saw it, my job was primarily to listen and occasionally ask a pertinent question, just as Jim Tenney had done for me. Usually those questions were aesthetic in nature, or specific to a technical detail of the work at hand. But occasionally I would raise larger questions. Like me, these kids had grown up privileged, and immersed in commercial pop culture. So I wanted to be sure they were really thinking about what they were getting into. "Okay," I might say. "You're smart. You're talented. You're ambitious. None of that will make you an artist. How will you overcome your gifts to make your life as a composer?"

That semester at Oberlin I hosted Jim Tenney, Peter Garland, and Kyle Gann to give lectures and coach performances of their music. The Oberlin Contemporary Music Ensemble premiered and recorded *In the White Silence*, and Percussion Group Cincinnati recorded *Strange and Sacred Noise*. It was an exciting time. But I was thrilled to return home, even in the middle of winter.

As we spent more time outside Alaska, Cindy and I had begun to notice that not everyone lived in the same rustic way that we did. And after living for a while in more comfortable quarters, I felt impelled to make improvements to our house in Fairbanks. I began by replacing the rotten old pine deck with a gleaming new expanse of Alaska yellow cedar. The new deck made us realize just how bad the whole house was. Over the next dozen years, whenever we'd saved up enough money, we chipped away at things.

We knocked out interior walls, turning all the tiny nooks and crannies into a single open space that felt much larger than it actually was. We raised the roof, changing the cramped little loft into a magical upstairs room. We added large energy-efficient windows everywhere, so the house was flooded with light. We installed a high-efficiency boiler and in-floor radiant heat. We designed and installed a stairway with no stringers and no risers that appeared to float right out of the wall. ("Like the homeowner," I liked to say. "No visible means of support.") We built a real cook's kitchen for Cindy, and a dining nook on an elevated platform surrounded by glass. Sitting in that space during a snowfall felt like being inside one of those old-fashioned holiday snow globes. Eventually we enclosed the entire bathroom in walls of frosted glass. The large stainless-steel showerhead was embedded in the ceiling, so the water seemed to just fall from the sky.

By the time all this was over, we had transformed a sow's ear of a cabin into a gleaming little silk purse of a house. We spent far too much money on these renovations, as I indulged my perfectionism and my architect/designer fantasies. But we loved living in that house. And although there were times when I should've been down at the studio rather than up at the house, playing contractor, it was a great learning experience.

Like homebuilding, composing music involves design, material, and work. The most successful designs are usually the simplest. And the best construction is usually the most transparent. No matter how much good work may lie beneath the surface, technique should disappear, leaving only the beauty of the material visible or audible.

It wasn't quite a glass house. (This *was* Alaska, after all.) But from any point inside or out you could see right through our house. There were no rooms. Aside from closets, there were no interior walls or doors. The entire house was a continuous space on three different levels. This design is a lot like the forms of my music, in which I imagine an entire composition as a single multi-dimensional sonority, transparent in form, harmony, texture, and orchestration.

Like the birch-and-spruce forest around it, our house contained only a few basic elements. Selecting the materials for the vertical surfaces was easy. All the walls were drywall, painted white. The windows and the exterior doors were made of high-efficiency glass (triple panes, low E, with argon gas). On the main floor we installed wood flooring. Since the bedroom level was four feet belowground, we wanted the floor to reflect as much light as possible. So we settled on pure white concrete, with a hand finish. The idea was to make things perfectly smooth with as little evidence of the mason's hand as possible. But perfection is impossible. And that's precisely the point. Ultimately every sweep of the trowel, every little gesture is visible. Those traces on the surface reveal the essential nature of the material and create the character of the finished floor.

After the concrete was poured, it was smoothed out with a screed. Then we waited until the material had dried enough to be worked by hand. The first round of trowel work took a couple of hours. We took a break, and then the mason went back to work on the finish coat. After a few minutes he turned to me and said: "We should leave it alone." His experienced hand and eye told him that the material didn't want to be worked anymore, that we'd get the most beautiful finish by walking away and letting it cure.

I learned a lot about music from that mason, as I did from the carpenters, plumbers, electricians, painters, glaziers, and other tradespeople who helped us build our home. The best of these workers don't force things. They don't call attention to themselves. They simply reveal the essence of the designs and the character of their materials. Although they strive for perfection, they understand that perfection is rarely attainable and isn't necessarily the best solution.

At the successful completion of a task my carpenter friend John Murphy would sometimes quip: "Perfect . . . but it'll do." Or as my friend Birch (the carpenter-poet) puts it: "Wholeness is better than perfection." I'm still learning this lesson every day, in life and in art.

Birch says that his least favorite part of construction is foundation work. It's difficult, time-consuming, and not immediately gratifying. It's also the most important part of the job. If the foundation is off, even by a little, the entire structure will never be quite right. So he always takes his time and pays special attention to the foundation.

I try to do the same with my music. Often, I spend as much time sketching and preparing the foundation for a new piece as I do composing the finished tones and rhythms, the "piece" itself. Having gone through the process of excavation, laying the gravel pad and pipes for ventilation, pouring the slab and building the block wall for the addition to our house, I now understand the importance of foundation work in a much more tangible way.

In the fall of 1999 Cindy and I boarded another flight south, to return for a semester teaching at Oberlin. I didn't want to leave Alaska, and as we passed over the peaks of the central Alaska Range, I was filled with an almost painful feeling of tenderness for the landscape below. A vision came to me of a piece—a *place*—where we could hear the elemental vibrations that are all around us all the time, just beyond the reach of our ears. I knew I couldn't fake this. Nothing could be recorded. It had to be *real*.

The Place Where You Go to Listen is a small room at the Museum of the North in Fairbanks. Inside this space the rhythms of night and day, the phases of the moon, the seismic movements of the earth, and the dance of the aurora borealis are transformed into sound and light. I began concentrated work on the winter solstice of 2003, and for the next two years I lived, breathed, and dreamed *The Place Where You Go to Listen*.

There are no familiar sounds in *The Place*, no sounds from nature, no musical instruments that we've heard before. Everything is synthesized in real time, on a computer, in response to inaudible vibrations in the world around us. In my one-room cabin studio, the brilliant young composer and programmer Jem Altieri and I worked side by side. Jem created the complex program that translates geophysical data streams from the real world into the musical world I was composing for *The Place*. I would share my notations with Jem—musical notes, tables of tunings, sketches on graph paper of the cycles of the sun and the moon, and my ideas for translating seismic and geomagnetic weather data into sound. We'd talk these things through, and then she would miraculously transform them into code. We would listen and discuss the results. I'd revise my notations, and Jem would revise the code.

This went on for months as, one by one, we developed each of the elements in the virtual choir and orchestra of *The Place*—the day choir and the night choir, the voice of the moon, the aurora bells, and the earth drums. Eventually we had all the elements integrated into a "flight simulator" connected to a multi-channel sound system in my little cabin studio. This allowed me to simulate any weather conditions, any magnitude of seismic event or geomagnetic (aurora) storm for any date and any time of day. I could accelerate the clock to hear how the sound might change over the course of a day. I could jump from winter solstice to vernal equinox to summer solstice, and hear similar conditions in different seasons. I spent countless hours doing this. I spent even more time listening to the sound of *here* and *now*.

For the better part of a year I left the flight simulator running 24/7. Each time I returned to the studio I'd walk through the door eager to hear how the sound had changed while I'd been away. Sitting there gazing out the window into woods toward the mountains beyond, I would ask myself: "Does this have the ring of truth? Does it sound, does it *feel* like this moment in this place?"

I love maps. A good map constitutes a score that evokes the music of the land, deepening our understanding of where we are.

Occasionally on camping trips I've used maps to help me find my way in unfamiliar terrain. Now I was making my own maps to help me find my way into this strange new sonic territory. Jem and I were mapping data—taking streams of numbers measuring geophysical phenomena, and making musical maps of the sounds in *The Place Where You Go to Listen.* The cycles of daylight and darkness became choirs of singing voices. The movements of the earth became rumbling drums. Geomagnetic disturbances in the upper atmosphere became shimmering bell tones.

When we began work on the aurora bells, I had in mind to orchestrate the geomagnetic data to sound like the aurora looks. I imagined audible forms that would somehow move in synchronization with the forms of the aurora borealis in the sky. Gradually it occurred to me that the magnetometer data and the aurora are two utterly different phenomena. It's true they're closely related (when the magnetometer readings are active, so is the aurora, and vice versa), but it's virtually impossible to find specific correlations between geomagnetic activity and the visible forms of the aurora. As my friend and collaborator the aurora scientist Dirk Lummerzheim puts it: "The magnetometers don't measure the aurora. They measure 'space weather.'"

The Place doesn't illustrate the visible. It doesn't amplify the audible. It resonates with the inaudible and the invisible. While we were working, a major geomagnetic storm occurred, treating people in the temperate zone to spectacular displays of aurora. In Fairbanks, we had dense cloud cover and snow, so we didn't see any of that activity. Yet listening inside *The Place* we could *hear* that storm.

The only way to experience *The Place Where You Go to Listen* is to be in that small room in Fairbanks. The sound of the piece is so complex and subtle that it's not possible to convey it on recording or an internet stream. I was so enamored of this new sound world that I wanted people who couldn't make the trip to Alaska to hear some of it, and I was eager to explore it in other ways.

When I was twenty-one, I'd encountered Henry Cowell's visionary book *New Musical Resources* (1921). In the chapter on rhythm, Cowell proposes nothing less than a unified field theory of music—compositions that encompass not only tonal harmonies but also rhythmic harmonies derived from the whole-number relationships of the natural harmonic series. As Cowell explained, what we perceive as pitch and as rhythm are just different parts of the electromagnetic spectrum. Pitch is simply fast rhythm (in the range of 20 to 20,000 vibrations per second). Conversely, rhythm is simply slower pitch. This was a musical epiphany for me. And ever since that first reading of Cowell, most of my music has encompassed three, four, or more different tempos simultaneously, in my search to create enveloping musical spaces and places. From time to time, working with computer-generated sound has allowed me to do this in a mathematically exact way.

Veils and Vesper is a set of four electronic soundscapes that fill time and space with enveloping atmospheres of harmonic color. These are my most rigorously formal pieces. They're purely algorithmic. Yet this is also perhaps my most unabashedly sensuous music.

The harmonies and melodies in *Veils and Vesper* are tuned to the prime-number harmonics 11, 13, 17, 19, 23, 29, and 31. It takes six hours for the complex web of tempos and rhythms derived from these same numbers to complete one cycle. The music encompasses a ten-octave range (extending above and below the range of human hearing) and a total of ninety polyphonic voices. The resulting fields of sound saturate the air so much that it's often difficult to distinguish one tone from another. They tend to meld together into rich, ambiguous sonorities in which the higher tones sound like harmonics of the lower tones. The timbres are clear and slightly breathy, like human voices mixed with bowed metal or glass.

Before I began *The Place Where You Go to Listen*, my longest works had been sixty to eighty minutes. Now I had one piece that was six hours long, and I was working on another that, in principle, would never end. It would also never repeat itself. Although I composed all the elements of *The Place*, exactly how events would unfold moment to moment was ultimately beyond my control.

For much of the summer of 2004 the world outside my studio was filled with smoke from wildfires all over interior Alaska. One night at about one o'clock, in the crepuscular light of the subarctic summer, Cindy, our friend Annie Caulfield, and I drove out to the Boundary Fire, which was sweeping through the boreal forest off the Steese Highway, some fifty miles north of Fairbanks.

As we crested the hills beyond the Chatanika River, the sky glowed with the color of wild roses. From high above, long fingers of virga reached downward—the rain reaching toward but never quite touching the earth. In the west a third-quarter moon hung, impossibly large, yellow-gray. We descended into the valley. The sky darkened. The ground was barren. The trees were black. Banners of smoke rose from the slopes above us. A fine mist of ash began to fall. As we moved deeper into the country, flashes of orange light appeared, one by one, like a hundred campfires scattered all around.

We stopped the car. Amid the flames and smoky light, the birds were still singing—the music of hermit thrushes surround-

ing us like the echoes of small bells, mingling with the murmurs of a stream rising from the darkness below. And another
sound—first breathing, then sighing, then clattering like stones
rolling down a talus slope—as a geyser of flames erupted from
the crown of an ancient spruce. We walked to the top of a steep
draw and found ourselves standing on the edge of an inferno. A
searing wind roared up the slope, showering sparks into the sky
above us. It felt like standing next to a waterfall, on the bank of
a dangerous river. With one more step we could be swept away,
consumed by the rising torrent of fire. We were frightened. But
we didn't move. The heat was intense yet somehow comforting,
the sound ominous and mesmerizing. The fire continued to flow
downslope, devouring the forest, moving inexorably toward the
stream.

We drove on, descending toward the Yukon River. Gradually
as the slopes fell away, we could see the edge of the smoke, hanging
like an enormous black knife low on the horizon. Beyond, farther
to the north, pale blue light stretched away into morning. A gentle
rain began to fall.

After that hellish summer, I relished the magic of the following winter. Interior Alaska is one of the best locations on earth
for viewing the aurora borealis. That January we experienced a
geomagnetic storm that produced maximum aurora. As I often
did, I worked late, walking back up the hill from the studio well
after midnight. It was cold, about 30 below zero. I poured myself
a dram of whisky and settled into the soft chair by the large windows in the living room. The third-quarter moon set about 1:30
a.m., and the fireworks began.

Every quadrant of the sky blazed with red and green light
moving in a breathtaking array of forms. And then I saw something I'd never seen in thirty years of aurora watching. In the
western sky a wall of red aurora shot upward, again and again,

like a rising waterfall of fire. Usually we see the aurora in vertical forms that appear to move laterally. These curtains were moving *vertically*, sweeping up and up again toward the zenith. The speed and intensity of this torrent was almost frightening, like a vision of the apocalypse.

At another moment the aurora was so extensive that I couldn't really see it—there was too little contrast. The entire sky was saturated with phosphorescent green, and although it was crystal clear, the photon mist was so dense that only the brightest stars and planets shone through the ghostly white light.

A week later, under the full moon, I sit watching stars—in the sky, and in the snow. The deep cold has pulled the flakes into large feather crystals that reflect the moonlight, creating points of light more brilliant than all but the brightest stars in the sky. Like the stars above, these snow stars form constellations. I watch them carefully. After just a few minutes, everything seems to have changed. I pick a particularly prominent snow star and sit very still, focusing on it intently. Before long, the star has faded and others have appeared. These snow constellations change much more rapidly than the constellations in the sky.

The next night I return to my snow-star gazing. Last night I watched them fade. Tonight I want to see them appear. Choosing a section of the field with no points of light, I watch until the first trace of light begins to emerge. At first, I'm not sure it's really there. But over the next two or three minutes it grows to become an intense particle of illumination, burning in the snow. Another two or three minutes later, it's gone—dissolved back into the diffuse blue-gray whiteness of the field. The entire life cycle of one of these stars is perhaps five or six minutes. With just a little patience I can witness the birth and life and death of entire galaxies. I look up to the sky and wonder about the scale of time concentrated in the points of light that touch my eyes from those faraway suns. Their light comes from the time before time.

In the summer of 2005, *The Place Where You Go to Listen* moved out of my studio and into its long-term home at the Museum of the North. Situated on the west ridge of the University of Alaska campus, the museum is a major destination in Fairbanks, attracting tens of thousands of visitors each year. That year was the final phase in the construction of a spacious new building. Each morning Jem and I packed our lunch boxes and went to work in a hard-hat zone. I was determined to oversee every detail of the work. I'd learned a lot from the multi-year renovation of Cindy's and my house, so I decided to be my own contractor.

When we began work our site was an unenclosed alcove at the edge of a much larger gallery, just above the main entryway of the museum. Our first job was to transform that alcove into a room. This involved framing, insulation, soundproofing, drywall, painting, and flooring. Once we had our own self-contained space, we began work installing the sound system—fourteen loudspeakers hidden in the walls and ceilings. We installed a custom-built bench, and a computer-programmed lighting system. We constructed the "brain closet," where the computer, amplifiers, audio interface, and lighting controls reside—soundproofed and hidden behind the interpretive text that welcomes visitors to *The Place.*

I worked on all these projects—as the contractor, as a laborer, and as the custodian. Work on the site didn't begin until I arrived in the morning. And I was the last person to leave every night. Still, my primary work was on the art itself. Although *The Place* had been composed in my studio, we now had to fine-tune the piece in the room. Jem and I spent countless hours listening to the sound, looking at the colors, and tweaking the master program. The installation work was grueling. But this part of the job was sheer joy.

My original conception for *The Place* was truly grandiose. I imagined this piece could be realized at any location on earth, and that each location would have its unique sonic signature. In *The Wind Garden* (2017), on the campus of the University of California San Diego, a choir of virtual voices echoes the dancing of eucalyptus trees in the wind. For a proposed installation in Venice, Italy, the cycles of the tides would've shaped the music. An unrealized work in Montana was to be tuned to the topological contours of a mountain meadow. This idea—tuning the music of a place according to its particular features and position on the earth—has stayed with me. Perhaps one day I'll have the opportunity to explore it in other places. At one point while I was working on *The Place Where You Go to Listen*, I realized that I was tuning everything so that *this* place—this room on this hill looking out over the Alaska Range—would be the most beautiful-sounding spot on earth. The same would need to be true, anywhere.

While I was working on *The Place*, I traveled down to San Diego to give a lecture about my work. After my talk, I had a drink with my close friend the percussionist and conductor Steven Schick. As we sipped our single malts, Steve looked me in the eye and said: "John. You have to stop apologizing for your music."

This got my attention. "What do you mean?" I asked.

Steve continued: "You're always talking about the mathematics behind your music. But you could take those same numbers and make them sound like hip-hop or country music. It's what you *do* with the mathematics that matters. You're always talking about Alaska. But it's time for you to stop thinking of yourself as an Alaskan composer. Your music has become its own landscape now. We care about your music because it grabs us by the ears, because it takes us to a place we haven't been before and lets us hear something we haven't heard before."

Every composer needs a friend like Steve Schick. And although my reflex was to resist, I sensed that Steve had a very strong point. Even as I was immersed in creating this piece that was inextricably rooted in Alaska, I was beginning to understand that my work was leading me beyond my beloved home.

The Place Where You Go to Listen is perhaps my most specifically "Alaskan" work. In a sense, it was a point of arrival—the summation of thirty years living in and listening to the north. In another sense, *The Place* was a point of departure. Making music that unfolds in real time with events in the real world would lead me out of doors, to make music directly in and *with* the landscape. In time this would lead me beyond the specific geography of Alaska, toward music as a means of more fully and deeply experiencing place—wherever we may be.

In spring of 2006, Cindy, Gordon, and I made our annual spring camp at our favorite spot on a high bluff above a glacial river in the Alaska Range. I'd been commissioned to compose a new work for the Anchorage Symphony. Gordon was my trusted musical advisor, and since he was a veteran orchestra conductor as well as a composer, I knew he'd have a good perspective on the possibilities for the new work. As he so often did, Gordon hit me with a zinger.

"That hall is big," he said. "Everything sounds small in there."

I'd had the same experience with the concert hall in Anchorage, and voiced my agreement.

Gordon went on: "There's a good sound system in there, all around the house. You should use it. Do something with electronics."

Once again, Gordon had hit the bull's-eye. I was off and running.

For several years I'd been combining electronic sounds and acoustic instruments in works for smaller ensembles. But *Dark Waves* was the first time I mixed electronics with the complex sonorities of the symphony orchestra. Sibelius observed that, unlike the piano, the orchestra has no pedal. In *Dark Waves* I wanted to create one. I began by composing a score for an impossible orchestra—hundreds of imaginary musicians who never needed to breathe, playing instruments capable of producing infinitely sustained sounds and imperceptibly gradual changes in dynamics. I produced that massive score, sculpting layer on layer into huge waves of sound. Then I added the human element.

The electronic sounds of my impossible orchestra were generic and impersonal. The sounds of the real orchestra would be specific and human. The instruments speak in different ways. The string players change bow direction. The brass and woodwind players breathe. They play at different speeds. They ride the waves. They bring depth and texture, shimmer and substance to the music. They give it life. Even so, in composing the score for the human orchestra, I resisted the urge to add any new elements. I tried simply to transcribe the electronic "aura" as best I could. I imagined the whole of *Dark Waves* as a single, complex, slowly changing sonority—a vast roiling sea of sound in which everything flows into everything else. At the central moment of the music, the waves crest together in a tsunami of sound that encompasses all twelve chromatic tones, spread across the full range of the orchestra.

At the premiere in Anchorage, and after a subsequent performance by the Chicago Symphony, several people remarked to me that the piece was too short. One listener told me: "I was just learning how to listen to it, and then it was over." I realized this was something I wanted to explore on a larger scale. Although *Dark Waves* is just twelve minutes in length, I worked on it for most of a year. Several years later, I would compose *Become Ocean* in just four months.

For decades my music had been inspired by the big world outside our closed doors. Yet it was almost always performed indoors, in the circumscribed spaces of theaters and concert halls. Then, while I was working on *The Place Where You Go to Listen*, I heard *Strange and Sacred Noise* performed outdoors, and everything changed.

The percussionist Robert Esler and his teacher Steve Schick organized a performance on a high bluff in the Anza-Borrego Desert of Southern California. Indoors, *Strange and Sacred Noise* sounds big, powerful, overwhelming, even frightening. Outdoors, a lot of it just blew away in the wind. In that moment I realized the time had come for me to step outside—to compose music intended from the start to be heard out of doors. The result was *Inuksuit* (2008) for nine to ninety-nine percussionists.

Making music outdoors invites a different mode of awareness. You might call it "ecological listening." Indoors, we seal ourselves off from the world and concentrate on listening to an array of carefully produced sounds. Outdoors, rather than focusing our attention inward, we're challenged to expand our awareness to encompass a multiplicity of sounds, to listen *outward*. We're invited to receive messages not only from the composer and the performers but also from the larger world around us. Hearing music outdoors, it's sometimes difficult to say exactly where the music ends and the world takes over. There is no single point of interest; rather, every point around the aural horizon is a potential point of interest, a call to listen.

My point of departure for composing *Inuksuit* was the image of the stone sentinels that the Inuit have built on the Arctic tundra for countless centuries. I wanted to create my own musical inuksuit, in the form of rhythmic sculptures for drums and cymbals. Even though they would be made of sound, not stone, I wanted my figures to stand up. So (during a winter interlude in Mexico) I sat on the beach drawing in the sand and stacking stones. First, I would draw a figure in the sand. Then I'd gather stones and pile them up. If a figure collapsed, I'd abandon it. If it stood up, I would draw it in my sketchbook, to be translated later into musical notation.

In *Inuksuit* the musicians are dispersed widely throughout a large, open area, each following their own unique path through the physical and musical landscape of the piece. The same is true for the listener. There is no best seat in the house. You may choose to root yourself in one location and let the music swirl around you. Or you may wander freely throughout the performance, following your ears, actively shaping your own experience, creating your own "mix" of the music. For me this relationship between music and listener simulates a human society in which we each feel more deeply engaged with the world, and more empowered to help change it.

As I composed with those standing stones in mind, I imagined each musician and each individual listener as a singular figure in a vast landscape. I thought I was composing a piece about solitude. It was only when I heard the first performances of *Inuksuit* that I realized it's all about *community*.

Fairbanks stands just shy of the 65th parallel north—a little more than a hundred miles south of the Arctic Circle. Living there is like living in two very different places, winter and summer. On the summer solstice, the sun dips just below the northern horizon for a couple of hours. Civil twilight lasts all "night," and you can see kids playing softball or read a book without artificial light at 2:30 in the morning. On the winter solstice, the sun rises two minutes before 11:00 a.m. At "high" noon, it stands only 2 degrees above the southern horizon— barely clearing the peaks of the central Alaska Range, before disappearing again at 2:39 p.m.

Over the course of the years, as the photoperiod swings from one extreme to the other, there is never any equilibrium. Inevitably, these bipolar swings of light and darkness found their way into my music and my consciousness. One side of the music was explosive and ecstatic. The other side was spacious and introspective, filled with contemplative stillness. I came to think of these as the expression of two very different minds—summer mind, winter mind. People outside Alaska would ask me: "How do you deal with the cold?" Invariably, I would answer: "It's not the cold. It's the *darkness.*"

As Cindy and I got a little older and as the pristine ferocity of the cold began to diminish, the subarctic winter darkness became more challenging. We began spending more and more time in a house on the Pacific coast of Baja California. Our friends in the nearby village and on ranches out in the desert call me Juan. Cindy is Cynthia. I like the respect this expresses toward my wife, and I've always loved the resonance of her given name. Cynthia is what I've called her ever since. In that house, over the next decade or so, I would compose *Canticles of the Holy Wind*, *Become River*, *Become Ocean*, and *Become Desert*. In the *Become* trilogy, I sought to bring my ideal of an entire piece of music as a single, rich, complex sonority to its fullest realization.

For me music is a lifelong journey of exploration that has led me from the songs of birds and landscape painting in tones, to elemental noise and making music out of doors. Throughout this journey, *place* and *space* have been constant touchstones. But what is this obsession all about?

In my early years in Alaska, I worked with the *idea* of place—imagining each new composition as its own poetic or pictorial landscape. Over the years, the music has become less metaphorical and more physical. The physical, acoustic, volumetric space—the place in which the music is heard—has become a fundamental compositional element for me. One of the first questions I ask myself when I begin a new composition has always been: "What are the instruments?" Now this has become two questions: "What are the instruments? And where are they located?"

Music is composed of sound and silence, in time and in space. As Einstein and other physicists have taught us, space and time are part of a seamless continuum. Or as Samuel Beckett put it: "Time has turned into space and there will be no more time."

The book of Revelation is filled with apocalyptic visions of the end of time. Yet even as human society seems to be hurtling headlong toward oblivion, I hold no dreams of escaping via messiahs or spaceships. Ultimately, I think I'm trying to compose home, a place to live. I want to *inhabit* the music. There, I hope to find at least momentary refuge from our restless traveling from place to place, our breathless rushing through life. My deepest longing is to be fully present, listening in the present moment, here in *this* world—the only home I will ever know.

| V |

They Were My People

I was lucky to have known them when I did . . . They were
my people . . . and I do not expect to see their kind again.

—JOHN HAINES

1

Gordon Brooks Wright

We are in the middle of nowhere.

All the other musicians of the Arctic Chamber Orchestra have flown off to the next stop on our tour of villages in the Yukon-Kuskokwim Delta. With only our backpacks, a duffel bag full of music stands, and a pair of kettledrums, Gordon Wright and I are here alone at this remote airstrip, waiting for the plane to return.

It is early April. The world around us is an endless expanse of white. After the long night of winter, the sun has come back to the north. The morning is resplendent, but the air is cold. So we stand on the south side of the little shack next to the airstrip, basking in the warm light. Everything is golden.

Gordon and I will share many such moments in the years ahead. But although I can't yet imagine what a touchstone this golden light will become, even now I'm aware that this is a special moment. I am living a dream. I am not yet thirty. Here in Alaska I have found my own Walden—a rough cabin in the boreal forest. I've met the woman who will be my life companion, and together we are crusading to protect this place we so passionately love. I've composed my first piece for orchestra. I'm playing percussion and my best friend is conducting as we bring the music back out into the land that inspired it, sharing it with the people who have lived here longer than anyone can remember.

Out here amid the snow and sunlight, the world seems filled

with possibilities as broad as the country around us. Standing here, I hold a vision of pristine landscapes protected from destructive human incursions, of music rooted deeply in those landscapes, and of a culture in which we newcomers learn from our Native neighbors how to live in deep harmony with this place. This is a vision that I share with the tall, bearded, moose-like man standing by my side.

Although I love Alaska more than any other place on earth, I was never all that enamored of Fairbanks. Even so, I chose this homely boomtown near the Arctic Circle as my hometown for three principal reasons: the woman I had fallen in love with was there, the mountains I had fallen in love with were nearby, and Gordon Wright lived there. From the moment we met, as I passed through Fairbanks between my wilderness travels in the summer of 1977, Gordon and I hit it off. It was clear we were going to become friends. But Gordon always had a plan, and I suspect that in fanning the flames of my passion to make my home in Alaska, he saw the potential for me to become part of both the musical and environmental activist sides of his life.

Gordon conducted a lot of my music over the years, and he gave me my very first orchestral commission. While still working full-time as an environmental crusader, I composed *A Northern Suite* for Gordon and the Arctic Chamber Orchestra. In those days I wrote my manuscripts with calligraphy pens and ink on vellum paper, which I would send down to a shop in Los Angeles for printing. I had just received the freshly printed and bound scores of *A Northern Suite* in the mail, so Gordon and I walked over to the student center at the university to have lunch and talk through the new piece.

As we sat down with our lunch trays, I realized I'd forgotten to get something to drink. So I went back for some orange juice. When I returned, I saw Gordon sitting with a puzzled scowl on his face.

"Uh-oh," I thought. "He's not happy with the score."

Then I noticed that he hadn't even turned to the first page of music. The focus of Gordon's consternation was not the notes but the inscription inside the title page—one of my favorite passages from a poem by John Haines.

"This doesn't make any sense!" Gordon protested. He read the words aloud:

"'*There are silences so deep / you can hear / the journeys of the soul*'... What the hell is *that* supposed to mean?"

Simultaneously flummoxed and relieved, I replied: "It's *poetry*, Gordy! It doesn't have to make sense ... Just go with it. Just listen to the *sound* of the words."

Apparently he did. In the years to come, Gordon became John Haines's biggest fan, amassing a collection of the complete Haines—seeking out every chapbook, every broadside, every limited edition of every poem and essay that the bard of Alaska ever published. And over the years, he also came to feel that sound rather than syntax was the key to making sense of my music.

For my fiftieth birthday, Cindy and I were in New York, where our friends Fred and Alexandra Peters threw a surprise party for me. And there was Gordon, jumping out from behind the couch with the other guests. Later that week, we heard a performance of my piece *Red Arc/Blue Veil* at Juilliard. Our friend and fellow Alaskan Steve Williams was with us. Just before the performance Steve leaned over and said (somewhat facetiously) to Gordon:

"I'm not always sure how to listen to John's music. Do you have any words of wisdom?"

In his most expansive tone, Gordon advised Steve:

"Just let it wash over you. Don't try to make sense of it. Just go with the *sound*."

In his midsixties, Gordon faced significant challenges. As he confronted his own mortality, he wrestled with regrets about the past and uncertainty about the future. We talked about this at length, when we were alone in the sauna, and on a series of float trips we made down the middle section of the Tanana River. But as he approached his seventieth birthday, Gordon told me that he felt as though he had achieved "a vast new plateau."

In April 2006 my sound-and-light installation *The Place Where You Go to Listen* opened at the Museum of the North. The culmination of almost thirty years' experience living in Alaska, *The Place* contains no sounds we've heard before—from musical instruments, or in nature. This is a world unto itself.

Gordon flew up from Anchorage to be with us. I stood outside the room, greeting visitors and chatting as they entered and left *The Place*. Gordon went in.

Just a few minutes later I saw him come out, and I thought to myself: "Uh-oh. He's 'been there, done that' . . ."

But Gordon was just coming up for air. He walked right over and told me that he was overwhelmed by the piece. He proceeded to explain to me the deep connections, the endless possibilities within *The Place*, and the implications for my future work. Then he went back in for more.

I was relieved, happy that Gordon liked it. More than that, I knew that he truly *got* the big picture of where *The Place* comes from, both musically and spiritually. Musically speaking, Gordon and I came from different planets. But we shared the same fundamental faith in the power of music and the sanctity of the planet earth, in which *The Place Where You Go to Listen* is grounded.

My last sauna with Gordon was in the fall of 2006. It was a Sunday night, with just the two of us. "Just like old times," we said. As always, we talked about the past, about how rich, how blessed our lives had been. As always, we talked about the future, discussing the details of our various projects, and our respective itineraries, working out when and where we would see each other next.

Over the course of thirty years, Gordon and I shared many memorable camping trips. The last was in May 2006. This was our annual "spring camp." But although the calendar said the season had changed, at 4,000 feet in the Alaska Range it was still late winter.

Gordon, Cindy, and I hiked into our favorite campsite amid driving snow. We set up our tents, grabbed a quick dinner, and ducked for cover.

Cindy was cold, so I snuggled up with her for a while in our tent. Then I bundled her into both our sleeping bags and went to check on Gordon. He didn't look well. His face was pale. His lips were purple. And he was shivering.

I brought him a cup of hot tea, got him into some more warm clothing, and began massaging his feet. They were ice cold, and the bulging veins in his calves had an ominous blue cast to them.

After a while, he began to warm up. I went back and crawled in with Cindy. But I was unnerved. Gordon had always been a pillar of strength to me. I'd never seen him like this, and I didn't like it.

The wind howled throughout the brief twilight night, but by morning, the weather broke. The sun came out, the birds came out, and so did we.

After breakfast, as Gordon and I strolled across the tundra, joking and chatting leisurely, his tone became more serious.

"I don't know how much more time I have left, Johnny . . ."

I didn't want to hear this, and I must've challenged his assertion so vigorously that he decided just to let it go. We moved on to other subjects.

The next morning, before I was up, Cindy and Gordon sat as they always did, sipping coffee and watching the country. Gordon tried again: "Johnny doesn't want to hear this, but I don't know how much time I have left."

Without missing a beat, Cindy replied: "You got enough time for another cup of coffee?"

"Yeah. I think so . . ."

Not much more was said. But the Big Guy had made his point.

By the early 2000s, Gordon had taken to shutting down his cabin in the Chugach Mountains above Turnagain Arm to spend his winters at the guest cabin of friends at Timber Cove on the northern California coast. But in 2007 he made a midwinter trip home to Alaska, to hear the premiere of *Dark Waves* with the Anchorage Symphony.

The week before, I fly down to Anchorage for the first rehearsal. My flight is fifteen minutes early. As usual, so is Gordon. Since I have no checked bags, I figure I've got time to visit the men's room and then grab a cup of tea for the road. I emerge from the terminal, still a few minutes ahead of myself. And there is Gordon, standing outside his little Toyota wagon, pretending to look impatiently at his pocket watch.

Damn, it's good to see him! It's been almost six months since our last time together in Fairbanks. We embrace, give each other the requisite raft of shit, and pick up right where we left off. We're both looking forward to enjoying another memorable time together.

Downtown, we have dinner with the group of donors who commissioned *Dark Waves*. Afterward, Gordon and I walk over to the Hotel Captain Cook and head up to the restaurant on the top floor, which has the best selection of single-malt scotch in Anchorage. He kids me about my highfalutin tastes, then defers to me to make the selection. I order a fifteen-year-old Glenfarclas and a 1991 Glenrothes. The waiter puts the former in front of Gordon and the latter at my place.

As always, our conversation is wide-ranging and nonstop. As we banter and prattle on, I nose my scotch, admiring its legs and its color. Eventually I get around to tasting it. After savoring the finish for a few minutes, I think about proposing that we switch glasses. To my shock and dismay, I see that Gordon's glass is empty!

In the time it's taken me to muster one wee sip, Gordon has summarily dispatched his full dram. I kid him about his bottom-feeder ways. But I have no doubt that he enjoyed this fine whisky every bit as much as he enjoys the rotgut from Costco that he sometimes brings on our camping trips.

Since he began spending his winters at Timber Cove, Gordon has told me on several occasions about a piece he intends to compose, inspired by that place. Whenever he speaks about this music that he hears in his mind's ear he waxes poetic, describing a vast nocturnal sea of sound—dark, surging, beautiful, and foreboding.

My response is always the same: "Gordy, that sounds great! You should *write* that piece!"

Tonight I present Gordon with his copy of the freshly printed score of *Dark Waves*. He takes a sip of my scotch, falls silent, and begins studying it.

After a few minutes, he looks up, smiles at me, and says: "Well. I guess I don't have to write my Timber Cove piece . . . You've already written it *for* me!"

The next evening, I hear the first reading of *Dark Waves*. The session is in a small, unflattering-sounding rehearsal room. The musicians aren't yet certain what to make of their parts, which are filled with long sustained tones and quavering tremolos, devoid of melodies or easily recognizable musical landmarks. It's clear that the piece will be a new experience for the orchestra. Even so, from the first tentative sounds I can hear that it's going to work. After all those months alone in the studio, this is a terrific relief. I catch a midnight flight back to Fairbanks, looking forward to the following week.

In the current draft of the score, the strings play continuously from beginning to end. Even though the piece is only twelve minutes long, this is likely to induce fatigue for the musicians. So I spend the weekend cutting "breathing holes" in the string parts. In addition to giving the musicians a little welcome rest, this should add subtle variation to the overall texture.

On Wednesday afternoon I board my flight back to Anchorage, excited about hearing the new piece and enjoying some time in the company of my best friend.

We arrive right on time. I haven't heard from Gordon in several days. I know he's had lots going on. And amid the flurry of revisions and last-minute preparations, I've been distracted. But Gordon is as reliable as a Swiss train. So I'm confident that he'll be standing there by his car waiting for me, just like last week. When I walk out of the terminal and don't see him, my heart sinks a little.

I call his cabin. No answer. I call the Anchorage Symphony office. They haven't heard from him. I call home. Cindy is out. After forty-five minutes waiting, pacing, hoping, I finally grab a cab downtown. On the way, I call Gordon's cabin again and leave another message. I have just enough time to check into my room and walk over to the concert hall for sound check and rehearsal. The session goes well, but I'm distracted, and my sense of dread grows. The moment the orchestra is finished with my piece, I'm out the door and back on the phone.

Gordon was planning to stay tonight with our friend the violinist Paul Rosenthal, so I call there. No one is home and I leave a breathless message for Paul.

Next I call my friend Mike Dunham, the arts editor at the *Anchorage Daily News*. I haven't had dinner yet, so Mike and I arrange to meet at the brewpub across the street from the concert hall. I call Bob and Dorothy Childers, who live near Gordon out in Rainbow Valley. Dorothy tells me they'll go right down and check on him.

I walk over to the pub. Mike is already there. We order a little food and wait. In a few minutes, my phone rings. It's Bob.

In a whisper, he tells me: "John . . . Gordon has passed away."

My eyes fill with tears. I tell Bob: "I'll be out as soon as I can get there."

As I put the phone away, Mike looks at me and says: "You look like a guy who needs a ride."

We make the familiar drive south out of Anchorage, past Potter Marsh and up Turnagain Arm. The night is clear and moonless. Icebergs loom in the dark, churning in the turbulent waters. We reach the turnoff and make the slow, steep, winding drive up the mountainside. We pull in and park next to Gordon's familiar Toyota wagon, tucked into its usual spot. We get out and walk slowly up the hill, through the tunnel of alders to his cabin. Through the large bay windows, we see the light of one small kerosene lamp burning inside.

Gordon had built the deck of his cabin around a beautiful paper birch tree that he couldn't bring himself to cut down. We find him lying there, curled up against that tree.

Inside the cabin are Bob and Dorothy, two other neighbors, and a state trooper. The trooper goes about his business quietly and respectfully. When he's finished, he officially "releases" the body to us.

For years, Gordon had kept his own coffin by the door of his cabins, first when we were next-door neighbors in the woods outside Fairbanks, and now here in Rainbow. It was always good for a laugh when you'd take your boots off or put them on, sitting on Gordon's coffin. The plain pine box was tailor-built by our friend the carpenter-poet Birch Pavelsky, and it made its debut appearance in 1980 at the Halloween concert of the Fairbanks Symphony.

. . . The lights went down, and a hush fell over the audience. Someone lit a candle or two. From the back of the hall four shadowy figures emerged, carrying an extra-long coffin. With deliberate solemnity the procession moved down the aisle, set the coffin on the edge of the stage, and departed.

Ever so slowly, the lid of the coffin opened. A hand appeared on top of the lid, and a towering caped figure emerged. Turning to face the audience, the fearsome apparition lowered his arm and opened his terrible maw to reveal iridescent yellow vampire teeth!

Leaping to the podium, he hurled a downbeat and launched the orchestra into Mussorgsky's *Night on Bald Mountain* . . .

Ever since that night, all those years ago, Gordon has told me that it was in this coffin that he wanted to be transported for the last time. I turn to the present company and remind them of our friend's wishes. And now, thanks to his flair for the dramatic, I will have the dubious distinction of being a pallbearer for my best friend—*twice*!

Gordon was a mountain of a man. And we have our work cut out for us, getting the man down the mountain. We lift him into the box, but he doesn't seem to fit very well. His body is frozen. Gently, tentatively, we begin to move his arms and hands, his legs and feet, easing him into the coffin. At first this seems a little grotesque. But I recall massaging Gordon's feet when we were out on the tundra last spring. And as we work, we begin to find comfort in tenderly touching our friend for the last time.

We realize there's no way we're going to carry him down that steep, snowy trail in the dark. So we place the coffin on top of Gordon's big *akhio* freighter sled and tie it down. We slide it across the deck. And somehow, we manage to lift Gordon's two-hundred-plus pounds down the steep, snow-covered stairway with no railing. At the bottom, we catch our breath before beginning the trip down the hill.

Gordon was very particular. He hated it when people would punch through the snow onto the margins of his carefully man-icured trail. So, all the way down the trail, when anyone falls off to the side, I mock-scold them on Gordon's behalf.

"Hey! Watch where you're going. Stay on the trail!"

We're certainly an unconventional wake. Hanging on to the coffin and the sled, some of us are hunched over, attempting to walk. Others are crouched and sliding downhill on our feet. It's not at all clear whether we're driving the sled, or the sled is driving us.

Amid our intermittent tears, the giggling begins. As we continue on down the trail, we begin to see how sad and funny, how solemn and ridiculous our procession is.

"Gordon's last sled ride!" somebody quips.

And full-blown laughter breaks out.

The trail becomes steeper, and the coffin gathers momentum. One by one, pallbearers fall by the wayside. As it accelerates to-ward the road and the ravine below, only Bob and I are left—the two skinniest guys, hanging on for dear life. As we plunge down the icy slope, I have a fleeting vision of the three of us—Bob, me, and Gordon in the coffin—sailing across the road and over the precipice. Yet we manage to hang on and dig in and grind to a stop in the middle of the gravel road, just before the edge.

Only in Alaska!

We load Gordon into the back of a neighbor's pickup truck and begin a slow motorcade down to the highway. As he wished, Gordon will be cremated in this plain pine box. As we wait for the van from the mortuary to arrive, the trooper walks over and says to us quietly:

"I didn't know this man. But the respect, the humor, and the love you folks have shown toward him tonight tell me everything I need to know about who he was."

Back in Anchorage at 3:30 in the morning, Mike and I stop at a seedy bar and raise a glass in honor of Gordon. Returning to the Captain Cook at 5:30, I fall into bed and sleep fitfully.

The premiere of *Dark Waves* seems to go well. But it passes in a blur, part of the waking dream of the past few days. Cindy has flown down from Fairbanks, and this afternoon we drive back out to Gordon's cabin for a potluck in his memory. It feels good to be in his place again, in the daylight, amid his friends and neighbors, telling stories and laughing.

As we leave the gathering, I linger and kneel down beside the beautiful birch where my best friend lay down for the last time. All the way down the trail, I weep freely. We return to Fairbanks on an early evening flight. To the west, beyond the Alaska Range, the sky glows a deep, burnt orange—like dying embers.

During the years we were next-door neighbors, each Tuesday evening after orchestra rehearsal Gordon and I would drive back to the forest and walk home together. When we'd reach the fork in the trail, Gordon would veer left off to his cabin and I'd continue on to mine.

One deep winter night when the temperature was in the 40s below zero, as I dipped into the low spot where the tamaracks grow, I heard a great horned owl calling:

"Hooo-hooh-Hoooo . . . Hooh-hoooh-Hooooo . . ."

I stopped. I answered. "Hooo-hooh-Hoooo . . . Hooh-hoooh-Hoooooo . . ."

The call came again, and I knew it was Gordon.

From that night on, whenever we walked home together Gordon and I would call back and forth. When I'd hear Gordon's last hoot, I'd know he'd arrived at his cabin. Then, a minute or two later, I'd step onto the deck at my place.

Each Sunday evening on my way to the sauna, when I reached the final turn on the trail to his cabin I'd stop and hoot. If Gordon was outside splitting wood or walking between the house and the sauna, he'd hoot back in greeting.

At the end of the evening Gordon would always stand on the deck and send me on my way. About the time I'd reach that turn in the trail, I'd hear him calling:

"Hooo-hooh-Hoooo . . . Hooh-hoooh-Hooooo . . ."

I'd stop, turn around, cup my hands to my mouth, and call back.

The years went by, and Gordon and I called back and forth countless times—in the forest at home, on camping trips in the wilderness, on busy city streets. Our hooting was a way of voicing our affection for each other. It was also a way of acknowledging our connections with the owls in the forest, and with all our relatives in the larger-than-human world.

I always imagined that Gordon and I would continue calling to each other until we were both old men. Then he was gone.

Gordon was meticulous about his schedule. We always kept each other informed of our itineraries, and after he moved away, we took care to plan our time together far in advance. For months we'd reserved a date when Gordon would be in Fairbanks for a performance by our friend the violinist Paul Rosenthal. The three of us were going to have a sauna.

In the weeks since Gordon's passing, I've been determined to keep this appointment. Paul agrees this is the right thing to do. So, after his concert, we walk the familiar trail out to Gordon's cabin.

We split wood and light the fire. We toast our friend, share memories, and catch up on each other's life. Then we head out to the sauna for a good, hot sweat.

In Gordon's stead I perform the duties of keeping the fire stoked, ladling snow and water onto the hot stones. But in his honor, we leave Gordon's customary *saunameister* seat open.

Paul and I are in and out of the sauna several times. When he's had enough, Paul retreats to the cabin. And I crawl back in for one final blast.

Ladling on the last of the water, breathing in the intense steam, I speak a few quiet words to Gordon. Thanking him for his faith and his friendship, I whisper my gratitude for all that we've shared in this small but powerful ritual space.

Then I tidy things up, crouch under the low doorway, and step outside.

The full moon is rising above the snow-covered spruce trees. As I stand bathing in the amber light and the deep stillness of the forest, a call rings out:

"Hooo-hooh-Hoooo . . . Hooh-hoooh-Hooooo . . ."

My heart rises. And I answer:

"Hooo-hooh-Hoooo . . . Hooh-hoooh-Hooooo . . ."

The owl calls back.

Months before Gordon died, I had another visitation—a premonition, perhaps.

After a long summer evening working in the studio, I walked up to the house around midnight. Cindy was already asleep, but I was hungry. So I tiptoed in, grabbed some fresh oysters from the refrigerator, and stepped outside to enjoy a delicacy in the subarctic twilight.

The oysters had been flown in from near Sitka, hundreds of miles to the south. I shucked a plateful, dribbled a little lemon juice, and started slurping. They were wonderfully fresh and meaty, redolent of the sea. As I savored the second oyster, I pondered how blessed we are, how rich and patient the earth is. I looked up. There on the branch just above me, not ten feet away, sat a boreal owl.

I didn't know how long he might have been there, watching me. A little embarrassed, I bowed my head and lowered my eyes. Slowly, cautiously, I looked up again. The owl was still looking at me, silent and implacable. Deep in the woods, a Swainson's thrush was singing. The owl turned and looked over his shoulder. Then he looked back at me with his intent dark eyes. I looked down.

I thought about slipping back inside to leave the owl alone, but I didn't want to frighten him away. So, moving as slowly as possible, I ate another oyster. Each time I looked up, the owl was still there, looking back at me. Now and then he would look over his shoulder—first to one side, then to the other. Then he would look at me again, and I would lower my eyes. This went on for quite some time. I ate another oyster, then another, and another, finally finishing my meal.

The owl and I sat there for a long time, looking at each other in the dusty light. The thrush kept on singing. The wind kept on rustling the leaves.

I looked down again for an instant. And when I looked up, the owl was gone.

Gordon was a violinist, and soon after he died, I found myself composing a piece for unaccompanied violin. As I worked, I had in mind three places in the mountains where Gordon and I had shared time together. I also remembered the small Aeolian harp I'd carried with me in the Arctic Refuge when Cindy and I had our wedding. The experience of standing on the tundra holding the harp on my head, listening to the wind, feeling the music flow out of the sky, across the strings of the harp, down through my body, and into the earth became a touchstone as I composed *Three High Places*. In this piece the fingers of the violinist never touch the fingerboard, and if I could've found a way to make this music without touching the instrument at all, I would've done so.

A few years later while I was teaching for a semester at Harvard, I met the extraordinary young ensemble the JACK Quartet. Although I'd composed for string quartet in larger works (including *Dream in White on White*, *In the White Silence*, and *For Lou Harrison*), I'd never had any interest in composing for the string quartet alone. Maybe it was the intimidating historical weight of the medium, from Beethoven to Bartók, but I'd never been able to imagine how I might make it my own. Hearing the JACK, I recognized that here was a new generation of musicians who could play anything I might imagine. And shortly afterward, when I received a commission to compose a new work for whatever instrumentation I wanted, I chose to compose my first string quartet. *The Wind in High Places* expanded on the solo piece I'd composed in memory of Gordon. And I would continue to explore this Aeolian music in my second string quartet, titled *untouched*. I was fifty-eight when I composed that first quartet. As I write now, I'm sixty-seven, and I'm working on my seventh.

It'd been clear for years that Cindy and Gordon were the two most important people in my life. Even so, I couldn't have imagined the impact of this loss. I'd never experienced grief with anything like this intensity. I resolved to honor it, to ride it out for as long as it might take. I tried to chronicle the experience in my journal. Over the course of weeks, I wrote a long, rambling letter to Gordon. I composed *Three High Places* in memory of my beloved friend. But I wasn't doing well.

I developed a persistent skin rash. My vision, which had always been sharp, became blurry, and my eyes began to sting all the time. Ever since taking a blow to the head during the construction of *The Place Where You Go to Listen*, I'd had a continuous ringing in my right ear. Now it became more disturbing. I fell into a deep depression.

Early in 2008, as winter waned and the sun came back, I began to regain my balance. Then in early summer, as they had the previous year, wildfires broke out all over interior Alaska. Cindy went to visit her mother in Minnesota. I stayed home. The fires intensified, and the smoke got so bad that I had to keep our un-air-conditioned house closed up, even as temperatures rose into the 90s.

Several months earlier a doctor had prescribed a benzodiazepine for me, ostensibly for the ringing in my ears. It wasn't helping. I was sleeping too much. And I'd begun seeing double. So I decided to go off the drug. The doctor who'd prescribed it was traveling abroad and unreachable. I asked another doctor, who said that because it was a small dose, I should be fine just stopping it. I did.

A couple of days later, cooped up in the house alone in the heat and the smoke, I became increasingly anxious. I went outside for a walk. But being immersed in the heavy smoke only increased my sense of claustrophobia. I was seeing triple around the edges of objects. My breathing was shallow. I began to panic. I called Cindy in Minnesota. She told me to call our dear friend Julie, who took me to see a doctor. And by the time we arrived, it was clear that I was having full-blown drug withdrawal.

Over the following months I clawed my way back to equilibrium by slowly tapering off the drug. Eventually we discovered that my vision problems were caused by rapidly advancing cataracts. I had surgery to remove them. Within a few months I had another procedure for secondary cataracts. Over the next couple of years, the dominoes began to fall, through a series of retinal tears, and finally two full-blown retinal detachments.

All this had made it undeniably clear that I wasn't young anymore. And without Gordon, life in Alaska just didn't feel the same. As the winter darkness descended again, so did the depression. By the end of that winter, I finally accepted that I might have to leave Alaska.

The author, right, and Gordon Wright

2

John Meade Haines

For John Haines, the homestead at Mile 68 Richardson Highway was the most important place on earth. The life that he lived in the forest on that hillside above the Tanana River gave him experiences that very few people in our contemporary world will ever know. Out of that life grew his singular poetic voice.

Many times I drove the seventy-odd miles from my place out to the homestead, to spend a night or two. Sometimes I would pitch my tent in the woods, or on a gravel bar down on the Tanana River. But most often I would sleep in John's writing studio, up the hill from the cabin. In the midnight dusk of summer, I would stand on the deck, listening to the sublime music of the hermit thrush. In autumn, when the first snows came, the cackling of geese would roll up the hillside from the river below.

As we walked through the woods or sat talking in the cabin, John would tell me about his early days—building the cabin, hunting moose, and fishing for salmon on the Tanana, about Fred Campbell, Billy Melvin, and other old-timers who had lived in the hills around Tenderfoot and Richardson Roadhouse. He told me the story of dismantling an abandoned trapper's cabin, sledding it down from the backcountry with his dog team, then reassembling it log by log on the site where it still stands, just behind his own.

John's cabin is small—a single room of perhaps three hundred square feet. Inside, along the north wall stands the woodstove,

fashioned from an oil barrel cut in half. Above it hangs a screen
for drying damp socks and mittens. Beside the stove, on the fire-
proof apron, John would set his boots. On the floor in the center
of the room is a two-by-three-foot hatch that opens to the "cold
hole"—a small cellar that serves as his refrigerator.

Along the west wall is the kitchen area—a small sink with a slop
bucket underneath, a few open cupboards, a diminutive table, and
a straight-back chair. There are three small, square windows. To the
south is an alcove, with larger mullioned windows facing the river
and the mountains. Here is another table, where John often sat to
read or write by kerosene lamplight. On the east wall, jutting toward
the center of the room, stands the bed. Beyond it, the Arctic entryway—a buffer zone from the outside air—leads to the single door.

Outside are a couple of lawn chairs, and a wooden cable
spool that serves as a table. Near at hand is a woodpile, stacked
against a wooden one-car garage. Tucked under the corners of
the cabin roof are the rain barrels, covered with framed screens to
keep squirrels and debris from falling into the water. Just off the
northwest corner is the smokehouse.

Behind the cabin, to the west, stands the trapper's cabin. Beyond it is the outhouse, a couple of storage sheds, and the trail that
leads to Gasoline Creek—where John sometimes got his drinking
water. Branching off that trail is a short, steep path to the tiny studio where John wrote, and where I sometimes slept. The room contains only a desk and chair, John's typewriter, and a kerosene lamp.

A few yards above the cabin, facing south, are the vegetable
garden and the potato patch; just to the east stands the greenhouse. Passing below is the trail that winds up through the birch
and spruce, into the high country where John ran his trap lines.
Not far along this trail is a short, steep branch that leads to the
"truth bench"—just big enough for two people to sit side by side
with a sweeping view of the intricate braids of the river, the vast

Tanana Flats, and the towering peaks of Deborah, Hess, Hayes, and Moffit.

During World War II, Japanese forces landed briefly on U.S. soil at Attu, the far end of the Aleutian Islands. Fear of an overland invasion provoked the rapid carving of a gravel highway across the wilderness of British Columbia and the Yukon Territory, to connect Alaska with the lower forty-eight states. After the war, following his time with the U.S. Navy in the Pacific, John and a friend drove the 1,400 miles of the Alaska Highway north from Dawson Creek. Here on the bluffs of the Tanana River, John found home.

Later that summer, his young wife, Peg, joined him. But with no desire to live the life that John had chosen, she returned to New York City in the fall, and John spent his first winter at the homestead alone. As he would remember in "Poem of the Forgotten":

> I came to this place,
> a young man green and lonely.
>
> Well quit of the world,
> I framed a house of moss and timber,
> called it a home,
> and sat in the warm evenings
> singing to myself as a man sings
> when he knows there is
> no one to hear.
>
> I made my bed under the shadow
> of leaves, and awoke
> in the first snow of autumn,
> filled with silence.

The following autumn John returned to New York, to resume his studies in visual art at the Hans Hofmann School. This
was during the peak of abstract expressionism, and some of John's
classmates and acquaintances would go on to make their names in
the art world. But John went back to Alaska. In 1954, John and
his second wife, Jo Haines, took up residence at the homestead,
where they lived for the next sixteen years, with little money or
news from the world beyond.

As he wrote in his memoir, *The Stars, the Snow, the Fire*:

> I remember things. Names, friends of years past, a wife
> far off. Last week I saw a magazine article on contempo-
> rary painters in New York City, photographs of people I
> once knew. I wrote one of them a letter, telling of myself
> here in the North. There will be no answer, and all that
> seems very far and ages distant.
>
> In that same magazine—or was it another . . . —I
> have read something of the politics of this nation and
> the world. Names again: Truman, MacArthur, Eisen-
> hower, a place named Korea.

John had returned to the homestead with the intent to continue working as a visual artist. Legend has it that he stopped
painting because his paints froze. But John told me that it
was the winters in cramped spaces with scant light that made
painting and sculpture so difficult that he finally decided to
give it up.

In the years that followed, living off the country in shared
solitude with his wife, John found his life's work as a writer. As he
recalled: "What I wrote then emerged with difficulty from a kind
of spell, one that I was reluctant to break, knowing that once I
did, nothing would ever be quite the same."

During this time, John wasn't completely cut off from intellectual life. He sustained not always easy correspondences with Robert Bly, Hayden Carruth, Wendell Berry, and other poets. He began publishing poems here and there. And in 1966, *Winter News* appeared. That slim volume by a largely unknown Alaskan was met with extraordinary critical response. When the Soviet Russian poet Yevgeny Yevtushenko visited the United States, he insisted on traveling to Alaska to meet John Haines. At sunset one evening in 1969—unannounced, and accompanied by a photography crew from *Life* magazine—Yevtushenko knocked at the door of the Haines cabin. The two poets shared vodka and conversation into the night.

Not long after that, John sold the homestead, left Jo, and moved to California.

Eleven years later John came home, and our friendship began. During our work on *Forest Without Leaves*, we spent a lot of time together at the homestead. Although he was now a renter, John felt as though he still owned the place—which in a very real way, he did. With or without the consent of the new owner, he began making repairs and improvements. Our friend Birch shored up the foundation of the original cabin and built the new writing studio and the smokehouse in which John cured delicious alder-smoked salmon. John was an accomplished gardener. He reclaimed his old potato patch and restored the large greenhouse he had built so many years before. In the summertime I always returned to Fairbanks with a cornucopia of freshly harvested squash, tomatoes, onions, and even melons. But John could no longer live off the land as he had when he was younger, and for the rest of his life he would come and go for temporary teaching posts and residencies outside Alaska.

In the late eighties John taught for a couple of years at George Washington University. This was the time when Pat Buchanan and Jesse Helms had declared their "culture wars," but social and political conservatives had not yet succeeded in severely curtailing public funding for the arts in the United States. The National Endowment for the Arts still made grants directly to individual artists, and working artists were regularly invited to the table to sit alongside the arts administrators on NEA grant-making panels. I sat on several of those panels.

Whenever I was in Washington, John and I would get together. We visited galleries and museums, and (in those days when they still existed) we browsed through the local bookstores. John loved to take me to his favorite restaurants—an Indian place in Georgetown, Italian and Ethiopian places in Adams Morgan, and his favorite British-style pub near DuPont Circle.

John was a very serious guy. To those who saw only this side, he could be downright intimidating. But he also had a very healthy sense of humor. One afternoon, walking from John's apartment to a nearby Indonesian restaurant, we passed a fellow walking a small lapdog on a leash. I harrumphed.

"Well, well. Isn't that a cute little stew dog? Not much more than a soup bone."

John snorted out loud, and then began riffing poetically about "stew dogs, pie pugs, and mulligan mutts."

When I returned home to Alaska, a postcard was waiting for me. On the front of the card was a jowl-faced bulldog wearing reading glasses and a visor cap, cigarette dangling from his mouth, apparently hammering away at the typewriter in front of him.

The card was addressed to "John Stewdog Adams." And the message, scrawled in John's inimitable hand, read:

"Noted mystery writer, Mutt Mulligan, hard at work on his latest potboiler."

Not long after that, I received in the mail a poem entitled "Das Kapital March." It began:

> When you're down and out in Washington
> And camping on the streets,
> Sooner or later you're bound to think
> Of where to get your eats.
>
> The kitchen doors are closing
> In the home you left behind
> And stew dogs, pie pugs and mulligan mutts
> Are all that you can find.

And so it continued, in a similar vein.

I came up with a little tune for John's doggerel, and shared it with him. But, thinking better of both our artistic reputations, I never brought the piece to performance.

The dog jokes continued for the rest of John's life. He would call my phone and leave a message composed entirely of growling and barking sounds. We exchanged doggie postcards and note cards by the score—the more ridiculous or obscene, the better. Mutt Mulligan and Stewdog endured to the end, even as other comic personae appeared.

I can't remember what precipitated it, but at some point John began calling me "Adam," and referring to himself as "Eve" or, better yet, "Evie." I still have the recording from my message machine in which he sang out discordantly:

> O, Adam, he trusted his Eeeeeve . . .
> That his heart she would never de-ceeeeve . . .
> But he found her awake
> In bed with a snake,
> With a holler you wouldn't be-leeve!

John's phone messages were the stuff of lore around our house. I loved coming to work at the studio to discover the latest installment of buffoonery from the bard. One time, in his most high-sounding Yeatsian voice, he left me this little parody of "The Lake Isle of Innisfree":

> I will arise and go now, and go to take a pee
> And a wee puddle I will make there,
>   just you wait and see . . .

Some years later, on my return to Fairbanks from a trip to San Francisco, John and I got together at his place for dinner. As a gift, I had brought an independent bottling of a single-malt whisky that I thought he would enjoy. After our meal, as we sat sipping and chatting, I asked:

"So. How do you like it?"

"It's all right . . . But it's more your taste than mine."

Later, as I was leaving, John moved to hand me the bottle of whisky.

"No, John," I said. "That's a gift. It's for *you!*"

"Well, okay . . ." he grumbled. "I guess you can drink it when you come back."

A few days later as I came into the studio and checked the answering machine, I heard this brief message from my drinking buddy:

"Uh, Adam . . . You got any more of that whisky?"

I howled. And years later I still chuckle every time I hear him in my mind's ear.

As he got older, John became an inveterate writer of limericks. Some of these were political in nature, and many of them were decidedly off-color. He published one or two in *The Ester Republic*—the local paper of the hippie mecca on the western outskirts of Fairbanks. And he kept threatening to publish a volume of what he referred to as his "light verse."

"Sure. Go ahead. Ruin your literary reputation!" I would say.

John would mutter something in reply. I don't doubt that he was quite serious about publishing such a book. But, much to my relief, he never did.

John never had much money. At the homestead he lived a subsistence life, with very little cash. And throughout his life, he rarely received a regular paycheck. So he was, to put it gently, frugal. Among his friends, it was a standing joke: Would Haines ever pick up the check at dinner? And yet on occasion he could be surprisingly generous.

Although he had given up his work as a painter and sculptor, John sustained a lifelong interest in visual art, and his musings on art history were points of departure for a number of his finest poems. On one of my trips to Washington, we visited the Phillips Collection together. There we enjoyed a major exhibition of paintings by the abstract expressionist Richard Pousette-Dart. However, the highlight of the day was the quiet interval we spent sitting together in the Rothko Room.

I was already passionate about Rothko. I had seen his works at the Museum of Modern Art in New York, and even at the Rothko Chapel in Houston. But that afternoon I was moved as I hadn't been before.

The room at the Phillips is quite small. The lighting is low. There are only four paintings, hung low, as Rothko intended. There's a feeling of confrontation. You want to stand back, but you can't—you'll hit the wall. So you're left with a choice. You can leave the room. Or you can submit to the paintings. John and I chose the latter. The museum was quiet that afternoon, and we had the Rothko Room largely to ourselves. We sat there in silence for the better part of an hour.

Before we left the museum, we stopped into the bookstore. John looked through the catalog of the Pousette-Dart exhibition. I picked up a large-format book on Rothko. It was a deluxe edition, filled with lavish color reproductions printed on the finest paper. I lingered for a long time, agonizing over whether to buy it. But the $100 price tag was beyond my means at the time, so I put it back on the shelf and we left.

A week or so after I got back to Alaska, the Rothko book arrived in the mail, accompanied by a lovely note from John. I was stunned. I hadn't said anything about the book to John. But he must've seen me admiring it and decided that I needed to have it. What's more, I knew that John couldn't afford this expensive book any more than I could. It, along with the note that accompanied it, remains one of the most thoughtful and cherished gifts I've ever received.

From time to time an auxiliary group of the Ace Lake Sauna Society—including John, Birch, and me, along with a few other friends—would get together at the home of the philosopher-fisherman John Kooistra, for dinner, drink, and a little reading aloud. Each of us would contribute something to the meal. I often made a big salad, and maybe some pasta. Kooistra would donate a special bottle or two from his well-curated wine cellar. Birch usually brought dessert. And, once in a while, John Haines would bring his specialty—moussaka.

John was a good cook. And his moussaka was mouth-watering. Together with a good salad and a fine red wine, it was a first-class ticket to gustatory nirvana. John prepared the dish the right way, cutting no corners, cooking each of the three layers separately before baking. In the finished casserole, the eggplant was toothsome, the custard light and moist, the lamb and the spices perfectly balanced.

As we lavished praise on the chef, John never missed an opportunity to remind us:

"I'm glad you like it. You know, it's an awful lot of work . . ."

This became a running gag. In innumerable life situations we found it amusing to quote John on this matter. Then one day Cindy decided to prepare moussaka for dinner. Knowing that she had a high standard to live up to, she did everything the right way. The result was truly delicious. However, as she served it up, she felt compelled to concede:

"You were right, John. It *is* an awful lot of work!"

In his last years, due to a heart condition, John's driver's license was revoked. Fairbanks is not a walking town, and the mass transit leaves a great deal to be desired. So it fell to John's friends to provide him with transportation. John Kooistra and Birch did a lot of chauffeuring. So did Cindy.

We had only one car, and at the time I was struggling with advancing cataracts, so I wasn't driving. But each Saturday after she finished her morning work at her office, Cindy cheerfully shuttled John to the grocery store and then to the public swimming pool for his weekly workout. This went on for several months.

One weekday afternoon, John called the studio: "Uh, Adam. Is Cindy at her office today?"

"Yes. She's there. Why?"

"Well, I couldn't reach her. But would you ask her to stop by on her way home?"

I did so. And that evening Cindy came through the door beaming, bearing a casserole dish full of moussaka, made for us by the master himself. We savored every bite.

For John Haines, writing was not a matter of literary achievement. It was an artistic imperative. John's work was a deep vocation, a calling. But his devotion to his calling came at great cost to him, and to those around him.

By nature, John was introspective and solitary. As a strong artist, he created a world of his own imagining, a world he inhabited, largely alone. At times there were discontinuities between John's world and the world that the rest of us inhabit. Living in isolation all those years on the homestead may also have deprived John of a larger sense of community, and contributed to what could sometimes be perceived as social awkwardness or insensitivity.

In his final years, John was profoundly hard of hearing. He was also fiercely proud. And what some people may have interpreted as aloof, brusque, or even rude behavior may well have been a result of John not hearing clearly, and being too proud to admit it.

There were many women in John's life. (His obituary in *The New York Times* observed that in reading Haines's memoirs we learn more about his sled dogs than we do about his wives.) He was legally married five times, and for all practical purposes he had six different wives. It's perhaps no coincidence that the two longest relationships of John's life were while he was living at the homestead—first in the 1960s, and then in the '80s. Both women were named Jo. John was a die-hard romantic, and away from the homestead, he had many love affairs. But he just couldn't seem to sustain a domestic partnership.

John's relationships with academia were similarly far-flung. Over the years he taught at many colleges and universities, including Sheldon Jackson College, Austin Peay University, the University of Cincinnati, and the University of Montana. The most satisfying of his forays into the academy were at George Washington University, and Ohio University in Athens. At both institutions he enjoyed two-year visiting positions, with cadres of admiring students. Not surprisingly, these were also productive times for his writing.

John's experience with the University of Alaska was not so felicitous. Although he was admired and celebrated far beyond Alaska, the state's primary institution of higher education never embraced the poet. For a couple of years, the Fairbanks campus had a chancellor, Patrick J. O'Rourke, who recognized John's stature and did his best to make a position for him. O'Rourke was the force behind the honorary doctorate that the university awarded to John. He also hosted meetings of a group of us who were working to purchase and preserve the Haines homestead.

Toward the end of John's life, a generous-spirited faculty member, Roy Bird, secured a modest adjunct situation for John in the honors program. (Roy was a large man, whom John affectionately called "Big Bird.") The pay was substandard, but the position allowed him to live in university housing for a while, and gave him a small office space. Most important, it afforded John the opportunity to work with young people again, and to enjoy some small measure of institutional respect at home. Yet it remains an enduring embarrassment and shame that the University of Alaska did not make a place of honor on its faculty for Alaska's greatest writer.

The enduring regret of John's life was leaving the homestead in 1969. In retrospect, his departure was probably inevitable. The more difficult proposition was trying to get back home again. In his later life John was filled with a deep longing to return to his earlier life at the homestead. But if the homestead was John's Garden of Eden, maybe that Eden never really existed except in John's imagination and in his writings. It certainly hadn't been an easy life, and perhaps what John really longed for was the sense of magic and discovery of those early days. Maybe he was trying to get back to that life with the hope of finding another *Winter News*.

Sometime in the eighties, John gave a lecture at the University of Alaska Fairbanks. (Tellingly enough, this did not happen in the English Department, but at the Geophysical Institute.) The title of John's talk was "What Are Poets For?" He later expanded it into an essay, in which he addresses the imperative for poets and artists to engage with the full range of human experience, including the major social issues of our times.

In the discussion that followed, a professor of psychology who was also a conservative columnist for the local newspaper voiced her disapproval of poets getting involved in politics, asking John:

"Why don't you write more poems like *Winter News?*"

Although he must have been nonplussed, John calmly reasserted his belief that poets and other artists have an obligation to address the complexities of the societies in which they live. The questioner wouldn't let it go, invoking Ezra Pound as a cautionary tale of what can happen when poets venture into politics.

I was outraged. And since that day I've taken up a personal crusade on behalf of John's later poems.

The writings of John Haines trace a lifelong journey of discovery—from his blood-and-bone experiences as a homesteader, to his deep reflections on art and history, to his last, expansive musings on the nature of the cosmos and the meaning of existence. In the body of John's work, and in English-language poetry as a whole, there's nothing else quite like *Winter News*. There's also nothing like "Meditation on a Skull Carved in Crystal," or the voice of the Cumaean Sibyl in "Night":

> . . . Leave to me
> this one sustaining solace—
>
> my night that has more night
> to come. To the sun that has set,
> whose dawn I cannot see . . .

Mute in my transformation,
And do not wake me.

Or "The Poem without Meaning," which begins:

We have been building it for
thousands of years, this emptiness
where grief is blowing . . .

In its beauty and simplicity, with its short verses and vivid images of the natural world, *Winter News* is easy to love. It addresses us directly, in terms we can understand. The later poems are not so immediately ingratiating. They require more effort to fathom. But if we're willing to do that work, reading them slowly and repeatedly, sounding them out loud, these poems reward us in surprising ways, as gradually we discover vast new horizons, deeper and deeper layers of meanings.

When John returned to Alaska in 1980, he seemed determined to recover the life he had left behind at the homestead. Yet even when he first arrived in 1947, the old ways of living off the country were coming to an end. By the time he came back home, all the old-timers he had known were gone. Alaska was booming. The new Trans-Alaska Pipeline was just over the ridge to the north, and the Richardson Highway, which had once been a narrow road farther down the hillside, now brought a growing stream of traffic whizzing past the cabin.

Although he was still strong, John was no longer young, and the rigors of survival by fishing, hunting, and trapping were now beyond his reach. A life that demanded such a direct hand in death had never been easy for a man of John's reflective temperament.

(He wrote in one of his early poems: "I am haunted by the deaths of animals.") And by this time, he seemed to have lost altogether whatever stomach he once had for those brutal realities of subsistence living. Besides, he had other work to do.

For several years John and his new companion, the artist Jo Going, shared life at the homestead. During this period, he wrote some of his greatest poems, and completed his luminous memoir. After Jo left the homestead, John stayed on for a while, until financial necessity and perhaps loneliness compelled him to leave. Eventually, John married again. He and his last wife, Joy, lived briefly at the homestead, but before long, they moved into Fairbanks, then to Anchorage, and finally down to Helena, Montana.

There had been many comings and goings throughout the decades. But when a group of friends met at the homestead to help John move out, we all knew this was the last time. John was despondent that day. He talked about suicide. We knew that he had guns, so we kept a close eye on him.

One by one, as cars and pickups were filled with John's possessions, they departed for Fairbanks. Finally, only John and I were left. I did my best to console him: "This is your one true home, John. It will always be. It will live on in your books. But in another sense, your work is now your home."

I knew that my words were grossly inadequate to ease the pain that my friend was feeling.

We walked to the gate, where the sign reads:

Richardson Homestead
Established 1947

I offered to close the gate. John wanted to do it himself.

It was time to go. But John wanted a few minutes alone. Although I was afraid that he might do something drastic if I left him, I felt I had no real choice: I had to honor John's request.

I got in my car and drove off.

At the top of the hill, out of sight of the homestead, I stopped. I waited there for what seemed like a very long time, my heart filling with dread. Just as I was about to turn around and drive back, John appeared, putt-putting slowly up the hill in his little Toyota.

Despite his deep ties to the landscapes of interior Alaska, John Haines was far more than a regionalist or a "nature writer." In his memoirs of the homestead, Haines evokes a mythical time and place. Reading those pages, we travel through a dreamscape inhabited by the spirits of wild animals, filled with the trials and revelations of life in a cold and distant country. His work is not nostalgia for the way things once were. It's a quest to see clearly, and to speak truthfully.

In the preface to his collected poems, *The Owl in the Mask of the Dreamer*, Haines reflects: "I am aware . . . of a prevailing somberness, of a tone that might be called elegiac. All I can say is that the author has seen life and experience in a certain way, has seen human history as it appears to him, and not otherwise."

For most of the time that I knew him, John was fit and active, appearing younger than he actually was. As he moved into his eighties, he began to show his age. His hearing became worse. He shrank physically, and began to look frail. His intellect, however, was undiminished. He still read voraciously. He still had the same silly sense of humor. And he could still recite poems— his own and those of others—from memory.

During a visit to the emergency room, John surprised a pretty young nurse when, in his boldest reciting voice, he began intoning the fifteenth-century Spanish poet Jorge Manrique:

Este mundo es el camino para el otro . . .

At eighty-six and in failing health, John was still John. Yet it was clear that his time was approaching.

John often joined Cindy and me for dinner or brunch at our house on Coyote Trail (which he liked to call "Corroded Tail"). Our last meal together was in October 2010. Cindy and I were about to leave to spend the fall in Mexico, and the winter at Harvard. John could no longer drive, so Sage brought him out and shuttled him back home. The four of us enjoyed the feast that Cindy prepared. Afterward, we sat in the living room as the light on the snow dissolved into glacial blue. As we had done so often before, we sipped a little single-malt whisky, and John recited a few poems for us.

As darkness continued to descend, we said goodbye. I told John that Cindy and I would be back in the spring. But he and I both knew this was probably the last time we would see each other, and we said so. As we embraced, I told John that I loved him. And he told me the same.

As the car pulled out of the drive, I waved. I walked back into the house and collapsed, weeping on Cindy's shoulder. Yet despite the sense of impending loss, there was nothing unresolved between John and me, and nothing more to be said. Our goodbye was as sweet and as simple as our friendship had always been.

John passed away in March 2011. Obituaries and tributes appeared in magazines and newspapers around the world. There was a big memorial event in Fairbanks, with smaller gatherings at the homestead, and here and there. Later that summer, after things had died down, Birch, John Kooistra, and I returned to Mile 68 Richardson Highway for a final quiet observance.

We shared a few stories and raised a dram of rare whisky to

our friend. We set the empty bottle and a memorial plaque on his table by the windows facing the Alaska Range. We climbed the hillside and sat on the "truth bench."

Then, carrying John's ashes, we descended to the river.

The author, right, and John Haines

3

I Do Not Expect to See Their Kind Again

For me, John Haines and Gordon Wright were the embodiment of Alaska, living with high ideals and without compromise, far beyond the boundaries of convention.

When Gordon passed away, I began to sense that the time for me to leave Alaska was drawing near. When John passed away, I knew that time had come.

John and Gordon were very different men. But both were essential role models for me. Intensely focused and fiercely dedicated to his life's work, John could be prickly and aloof. Expansive in his interests and enterprises, Gordon was affable and charming.

From John, I learned how to live without compromise as an artist. From Gordon, I learned how to live more fully as a man. I am still learning from both of them. And I expect this learning to continue as long as I live.

Almost every day, as I ponder a problem or possibility, I find myself wondering: "What would Gordon think about this?" Or, in my mind's ear, I hear John's rich baritone voice intoning a phrase from one of his poems, right when I need it.

Through their friendship, their lives, their work, and their spirits, Gordon Wright and John Haines continue to challenge, comfort, and inspire me.

They were my people.

| **VI** |

Leaving Alaska

The trail is barely visible, unless you know it's there.

I step off the dirt road and into the woods. The ground receives me with the familiar caress of home. I float down the trail—my feet intimately familiar with each little dip and rise, each stray root protruding from the ground.

The trail is worn smooth. But on both sides the powder-light glacial soil is blanketed with a thin layer of moss and lichen, low-bush cranberry, and Labrador tea. For one week each spring, the color and perfume of wild roses fill these woods. There are paper birches and spruce, both black and white. But the predominant tree here is *Populus tremuloides*   quaking aspen.

Up ahead, through the trees, the rough-cut siding of the studio comes into view. Before long, I slip around the aspen that juts into the trail, and step up onto the deck. I walk around to the front of the studio and stand there in the sun gazing south, downhill across the Tanana Flats toward the peaks of the central Alaska Range. Behind me I feel the forest sweeping north to the Yukon River, across the Arctic Circle and on to the solitary peaks of the Brooks Range.

This is the boreal forest. This is my home.

I walk to the back stoop and open the door. As I step inside and close it, I feel as though I'm leaving the rest of the world behind.

I hang my hat on the wooden peg next to the hat of my best

friend. Although he no longer walks these woods in the flesh, Gordon is always with me in spirit. I pull off my boots and put on my slippers. I am ready to go to work.

For the better part of three decades now, this sixteen-by-twenty-foot one-room cabin has been the center of my world.

The bookshelves that line the wall to my right hold my personal reference library. Here are some of the first scores I ever bought—Stravinsky's *The Rite of Spring*, and *Déserts* by Edgard Varèse. Here, alongside the scores of *Parsifal* and *Boris Gudonov*, is Debussy's opera *Pelléas et Mélisande*, a gift to myself for my thirtieth birthday.

Here is the complete, mint-condition set of the lavishly produced 1960s and '70s publication *Source: Music of the Avant Garde*, a treasured gift from Gordon. Here, too, are the scores of *The Conquest of Mexico* and many other works by my friend Peter Garland, along with my collection of *Soundings*—the journal of scores that he published throughout the 1970s and '80s.

Here are the books that have influenced me most deeply as a composer: *New Musical Resources* by Henry Cowell, John Cage's *Silence*, and Lou Harrison's diminutive but invaluable *Music Primer*. Here is Harry Partch's *Genesis of a Music*, and *On the Sensations of Tone* by Hermann von Helmholtz. Here are the books of poetry, essays, and memoirs by my dear friend John Haines, personally and sometimes quite irreverently inscribed by the author. Here are *The Odyssey*, *Beowulf*, and *Gilgamesh*. Here is *Moby-Dick*. Here are John Muir's *Travels in Alaska*, and *Arctic Dreams* by Barry Lopez. And here is *Walden*—the book that more than any other inspired the course of my life.

Here, too, are recordings that are landmarks of my life in music. Here are my original Beatles records, and LPs by Frank Zappa. Here are the Mississippi Delta bluesmen, *A Love Supreme* by John Coltrane, and Ornette Coleman's *Free Jazz*.

Here is *The Music of Edgard Varèse* (volumes 1 and 2), which first opened my ears to a strange and exciting new realm of musical possibilities. And here are the recordings of Javanese and Balinese gamelan, Japanese Noh, Kabuki, and gagaku, Indian classical music, African drumming and xylophones, which opened up for me the whole world of music beyond Western culture.

Here is the first recording of Harry Partch's *Delusion of the Fury*. Here, on LP and in two different CD editions, are the complete *Studies for Player Piano* by Conlon Nancarrow, and here is the *Missa Prolationum* of Johannes Ockeghem, an astonishing work from five hundred years before Nancarrow that explores a similar multi-dimensional concept of musical time.

Here are the symphonies of Sibelius and Bruckner, which I've come to in recent years. And here is *Morton Feldman: The Early Years*, the record that convinced me in my teens that this was what I wanted to do with my life.

Here are recordings of the interviews I conducted with Feldman and James Tenney, with Lou Harrison, Dane Rudhyar, and many other composers for the radio series I produced in the 1980s. Here are cassette tapes, given to me by those composers, of works of theirs that are still not widely available.

And here are recordings of my own music—performances and rehearsals, improvisations and sketches—dating back to the 1970s. Sometime in the early 2000s, while organizing things in the studio, I came across a box of these old reel-to-reel tapes of some of my earliest work and decided to transform them into a completely new electro-acoustic work titled *the place we began.*

Here are the DAT field recordings that I made over the years, all over Alaska: the thunder of glaciers crashing into the sea, the ethereal drones of Aeolian harps on the tundra, the haunting calls of swans, cranes, and loons, and the startling percussive music of walrus grunting, knocking, and chiming underwater.

Some of these recordings found their way into *Earth and the Great Weather*—my "sonic geography of the Arctic"—and, later, into *Ilimaq* ("Spirit Journey") for solo percussion and recorded sound-scapes. And I imagine that some of these recordings may still find their way into works yet to come.

Here, too, are the instruments. Here is the Aeolian harp that provided the music for Cynthia's and my wedding ceremony in the Arctic Refuge. Here are the woodblocks and temple bells that belonged to John Cage (which came to me as a gift, after his death)—each one bearing a small piece of cloth tape with "CAGE" written neatly in his distinctive all-caps.

Here is the Inupiat frame drum that a friend made for me, and the full set of tuned gongs that another friend brought from Thailand. Here is my father's silver cornet, on which he used to play "Sugar Blues," and which I played in the grade school band. Here is the black leather cymbal case with the 14-inch hi-hat cymbals and the 16-, 18-, 22-, and 24-inch Zildjians from my rock drummer days.

Hanging in one of two large south-facing windows is a small crystal globe that sometimes catches the low-angle winter sun-light and sprinkles prismatic colors around the room. In one of the smaller eastern windows stands a chambered nautilus that was a gift from my friend the composer and musicologist Kyle Gann.

On the sill of the tiny corner window high on the western wall perches an oriole nest that Barry Lopez gave me. Woven into the dense fabric of moss and twigs are long strands of cassette tape. In the note that accompanied it, Barry wrote:

"*songbirdsongs*, no doubt. But where do they buy the tapes?"

In the tall filing cabinets to my left are hundreds of such notes and letters from composers and writers, conductors and record producers, musical colleagues and my dearest friends.

Here are letters of deep reflection from Barry about our obligations as artists, and our parallel paths working in different artistic disciplines. Here are colorful and humorous diatribes from Peter Garland about the sorry state of politics and music in the USA. Here are folders full of affectionate cards, notes, and letters from Gordon, along with detailed notes from rehearsals of works that he commissioned from me and premiered with the Fairbanks Symphony and the Arctic Chamber Orchestra.

But the largest collection of papers is from John Haines. In several running feet are detailed letters and notes from our year working together on the cantata *Forest Without Leaves*. Here are drafts of many other poems and essays, earnest letters and bawdy cards sent from John's residencies and travels in Montana, Ohio, Massachusetts, Tennessee, Washington State, and Washington, D.C., from Anchorage, from his homestead on the Richardson Highway, or from just down the hill when he was living in Fairbanks.

The correspondences in these cabinets are more than records of friendships. Now, in these days of continuous e-mail chatter and instant "messaging," they are relics of a bygone era.

In the decade that I lived alone, down in the black spruce forest several miles from here, I would roll out of bed in the morning, crawl down the ladder from the sleeping loft, and find myself standing in the middle of my work. I loved it. And I couldn't imagine living any other way.

I'd never had a separate dedicated space for composing. But as soon as I had this one, I couldn't imagine how I'd ever gotten anything done before. Now there would be no more casual wandering around, into and out of my work. No more getting up from the piano or the writing desk to putter around in the kitchen or the storage shed. Now when I went to the studio, I went there for one purpose only: to work.

My walk to and from the studio became a cherished daily ritual. As I walked down the hill and into the woods, I gradually put down whatever quotidian matters occupied my thoughts, and by the time I opened the door and entered the studio, I was ready to work.

At the end of an intensive work session, as I walked back up the hill, my mind would slowly zoom back out, giving me a broader perspective on the work I'd been doing. On many occasions, a problem I'd been struggling with for hours would suddenly resolve itself. Some of my best work happened on my short walk between the studio and the house.

As a composer, I wholeheartedly endorse the notion that all the arts aspire to the condition of music. Yet I also have a chronic case of painter envy. I've always envied the hands-on relationship that painters and sculptors have with the materials of their art, the way they can get paint and clay on their clothes and under their fingernails.

Two of my favorite films are *Painters Painting*—shot in the studio with Robert Rauschenberg, Jasper Johns, Helen Frankenthaler, Willem de Kooning, and other great American artists— and, more recently, *Gerhard Richter Painting*. I love watching visual artists at work. And I've always dreamed of a big, bright open studio space in which to make my music.

But what makes those art studios so alluring? Is it the tools and the materials? Is it the spaces themselves, the high ceilings and the abundant light? Is it the quiet and the sense of solitude?

Just what is it that makes a studio a studio?

Artists are workers, and our studios are our workshops. But as helpful as it is to have a good workshop, what ultimately creates a studio is the presence of the artist at work.

In the southeast corner of my studio, in front of one of the large windows, stands the piano. It's a lovely baby grand that a friend and neighbor sold to me for far too little when she left Alaska. It's too good an instrument for me. But I've done my best to give it a good home. And although my piano playing is marginal at best, it's been an essential tool for my work.

Running along the other big window is the worktable. Like most composers today, I use a computer and loudspeakers for creating scores and for working directly with electronic sounds. In recent years I've returned to composing more with pencil and paper. In part this is a response to changes in my eyes. It's a way of fighting back, reasserting that my vision is still fully functional. But it's more than that. I love the feeling of a good, sharp pencil gliding across high-quality paper. Like working at the piano, working on paper keeps me more directly in touch with the physical reality of the music.

Although they're only a few feet apart, each of my workstations embodies a different mind-set, a different way of regarding the music. Working on paper I can make large, sometimes intricate formal structures. But as fascinating as they may be, the notes I'm writing are not music. They're merely symbols. And the piano puts me back in touch with the sound of the music. So I find myself moving freely back and forth between table and the piano. And, as with my walk between the studio and the house, I've experienced numerous little musical epiphanies in this short distance between the piano and the desk.

Behind me as I work are the long filing cabinets that line the north wall of the studio, filled with scores and performance parts, manuscripts and sketches, notebooks and journals spanning more than forty years.

It was in this room that *Earth and the Great Weather* and *Dream in White on White* were born. Here, in the five years following the death of my father, I composed *Clouds of Forgetting, Clouds of Unknowing*. Here, after the death of my mother, I composed *In the White Silence*. And here I completed the memorial trilogy that I hadn't set out to write by composing *For Lou Harrison*.

It was here that my spacious, eventless "color field" pieces unfurled themselves—*The Light That Fills the World, Dark Wind, The Farthest Place,* and *The Immeasurable Space of Tones*. Here, over the course of several years, I worked up the courage to compose *Strange and Sacred Noise*—a brutally elemental cycle of percussion quartets. Here, with *Among Red Mountains* and later with *Nuntaks*, I finally discovered a way of composing for solo piano that felt like my own.

Here I composed *Red Arc/Blue Veil*—the first time I combined acoustic instruments with an "aura" of electronically processed sounds derived from recordings of the same instruments. Here, for my friend Steven Schick, I composed another radically severe work, *The Mathematics of Resonant Bodies*, for solo percussion and electronic aura. And here I composed *The Light Within* and *Dark Waves* for orchestra and electronic sounds.

In this room I conceived and designed another room that now stands a few miles from here. In the year before my assistant Jem Altieri and I moved into the Museum of the North to install *The Place Where You Go to Listen*, I spent innumerable hours here in the studio fine-tuning the computer-generated sounds of *The Place*—listening to them in every season and time of day, in all kinds of weather and light—to test whether they had what I call "the ring of truth."

These and many other works were made here. This small cabin has been the birthplace of the major part of my life's work.

Over the decades people would sometimes ask me: "Do you ever think about leaving Alaska?"

In my twenties and thirties, my stock reply was: "No. I wasn't born here. But my life really began in Alaska. And I imagine I will die here."

In my forties, I found myself offering a new answer to the question: "Sure. Sometimes I think about leaving Alaska. But I have the greatest studio in the world. How could I leave that?"

As we moved into our fifties, Cynthia and I began to entertain the possibility that one day we might try living somewhere else, and as we talked about this with our friends, a new question came up:

"Aren't you worried that if you leave Alaska, you'll lose your inspiration?"

Usually I would wave this off with a confidently dismissive "Nah!"

But the truth is, I *was* worried.

As a young man, I had come north with high ideals and out-sized dreams. Up here, unfettered by competitive careerism, I felt free to follow the music wherever it might lead me. In Alaska I had discovered music that I might not have found in any other place. And I wasn't at all sure that I would feel a similar sense of possibility anywhere else.

But which came first, Alaska or the music?

Some years ago I was invited to compose a new work for percussion ensemble. The commissioners may have expected something like my big, noisy percussion music in *Earth and the Great Weather* or *Strange and Sacred Noise*. But for some reason I remembered a quiet little piece I'd begun thirty-two years before, when I was a student at CalArts.

As I played through my old sketches at the piano, I was surprised by how much they sounded like my current music. The open harmonies, spacious textures, and sense of suspended time in this music seem to evoke a certain northern atmosphere. Yet it was composed two years before I came to Alaska.

I was drawn to Alaska by the land itself and by my own desire, in life and in my art, for certain qualities that Alaska represents. And living here for much of my creative life, I came to measure my own work and everything we human animals create against the overwhelming presence of this place. I know that my music would not be the same had I not made my home here. The influence of Alaska on my creative life is immeasurable.

Yet over the years as my work matured, its "Alaskan" qualities gradually became less overt and more deeply assimilated into the music. I began to feel that my music was no longer *about* place, but had in a real sense become a place of its own.

Because Alaska is such a powerful place, it may influence artists who live here more directly than geography influences artists in many other places. But as global climate change continued to accelerate, my personal vision of Alaska as a world apart was challenged in an inescapable way, and I felt a growing imperative to expand my music to embrace a broader vision of the world.

Eventually, perhaps inevitably, the time came to leave Alaska.

My two closest friends, Gordon and John, had passed away. Other friends had left. And the vision we'd shared of an ecological Utopia in Alaska had faded. The politics of the state had become increasingly strident. And even as so-called reality TV perpetuated the mythology of the Last Frontier, it had become painfully evident that the frontier was gone.

Even sadder to witness was the accelerating reality of climate change in Alaska, the transformation we began to witness at the turn of the millennium. In our last decade here, the summers began to swing from one extreme to the other. A summer of vast wildfires all over the north would be followed by a summer of seemingly incessant rain. The first snows of autumn, which we could always expect in September, now came as late as the end of November. Spring breakup, which used to arrive suddenly and explosively in May, now became a slow meltdown, beginning as early as March. Winter temperatures became dramatically milder, and our subarctic winters had lost the pristine cold and deep stillness they once had.

At the same time that these changes were becoming undeniable, the trouble I'd begun to develop with my eyes made the long winter nights I'd relished for so many years increasingly difficult. After the second successive winter of black depression, it was clear that I had to leave.

Cynthia and I agonized over this. We had both come to Alaska in our twenties and lived here all our adult lives. Our life's work and our most fundamental sense of who we *were* was so deeply identified with this place that it was difficult for us to imagine what we might do and who we might *be* outside Alaska.

It seemed unlikely that anything could ever match the heady mix of idealism and romance we had shared in our youth. But after much soul-searching and many long conversations, we finally resolved that as we entered our sixties, we were ready to take a leap and embark on a grand new adventure.

We began spending more and more time in New York City, and in the desert outback of Mexico. In Mexico any lingering fears I had about losing my inspiration soon disappeared, amid the excitement of learning a new landscape—new weather, new light, new plants, and new birdsongs—in the Sonoran Desert at the edge of the Pacific. There I've composed the concert-length choral work *Canticles of the Holy Wind*, *Become River* for chamber orchestra, and my largest symphonic works to date, *Become Ocean* and *Become Desert*.

Cynthia and I sold our house in Alaska, and the ten acres around it. We also sold the land over in Canada where we'd dreamed of building an idyllic retreat. But we kept my studio.

With the proceeds from the sale of our house, we decided to buy an apartment in New York. It was a small place—a third-floor walk-up, not very fancy, and a little reminiscent of our early days in Alaska. We called it our "urban cabin." This was scary, but exciting. And we reasoned that if it didn't work out for us, we could always sell it.

But would I be able to compose in New York?

The answer turned out to be "Yes."

In the first year of our urban adventure, working in the living-room kitchen area as my studio, I completed *Sila: The Breath of the World*—an hour-long orchestral work that premiered at Lincoln Center. I also began and completed another concert-length work, titled *Ten Thousand Birds*, and I composed my second string quartet, *untouched*.

We moved into that first apartment on Cynthia's birthday. Exactly a year to the day later, we moved a block away into a new place, where I had a small but lovely room for my studio. Less than a year after that, drawn by open views, abundant light, and large terraces, we moved up to the top floor. The apartment is small, and I'm forced to work in the one and only bedroom. I've been productive there. Yet I've discovered that there's a certain kind of work that I just can't do in New York.

For that we go to the desert. We don't yet have a house of our own in Mexico. But we do have a truck—with Alaska license plates, of course. In the back of the truck are a folding table and chair, and a portable writing desk. Out in the desert, wherever we decide to stop, I set up in the shade of a cardón cactus or a mesquite tree. And there is my *plein air* studio. I also employ the same setup on the patio of the house we've rented now and again over the past decade.

In time I suspect I will feel the need for a larger, more permanent studio. But for now, with a small space in Harlem and a truck in the desert, I seem to have everything I need to do my work.

Alaska is still home, and it always will be. But I now feel at home in several places. Wherever my wife is, that's home. And the music itself has become a kind of home for me.

As we were preparing to sell our house and land in Alaska, Cynthia and I kept in mind the cautionary tale of our friend John Haines.

I remembered well that in 1947, at the age of twenty-three, John had carved his homestead out of the woods on a bluff above the Tanana River. For twenty-five years he lived there, eking out a living from fishing, hunting, and trapping, and writing the slim but singular book of poems *Winter News*. Following the publication and the overwhelming critical reception of his book, John decided to sell the homestead and leave Alaska. In the years that followed, to his dying day, selling the homestead was the defining regret of John's life.

The Haines homestead is 160 acres and stands face-to-face with the towering presence of Mount Hayes and the other peaks of the central Alaska Range. My little studio sits on just five acres in the "suburban bush," eighty miles farther north from the mountains, and just a dozen miles from downtown Fairbanks. Even so, this is the place where my music came of age, and where I composed many of my best works. And Cynthia and I were determined to learn from John's mistake.

We told ourselves that the studio would be our safety net. If things didn't work out for us "Outside" (as we provincial Alaskans refer to the rest of the world), we could always come back home and build a house somewhere on the five acres around the studio.

By now, I don't imagine that will happen. More likely is that
from time to time we will return home, and I will once again
work for a while in my old studio. For now, I take comfort simply
knowing it's still here, waiting for me to walk down the trail and
open the door.

The author and Cynthia Adams

| VII |

Walking Home Again

I am walking through a stunted spruce forest, walking home again.

How many times have I traveled this trail, in boots or snow-shoes, with a load on my back, hauling my sled behind me? I could've walked the entire mile and a half without any light, which sometimes I did.

The sighing of the ground, the softness underfoot is familiar. The spruce-scented air is comforting. But things have changed. All along the way there are deep ruts filled with standing water, and large sinkholes have appeared throughout the forest.

I reach the spot where the little stream used to cut neatly through the carpet of moss. Now it spreads out in all directions. The boardwalk is sinking, and the tilted spruce tree that we used to stoop underneath, I now step over. Soon it will fall into the water. As the permafrost continues to melt at an accelerating pace, this stunted forest—the dark taiga—will eventually disappear. I wonder what will take its place, and who may be here to see it.

I reach the turnoff to Gordon's cabin. I remember standing here on a bitter-cold evening, whooping out loud at the aurora borealis. How many times did we say good night here? In the twenty-five years since I moved out of these woods, I've turned here many times and walked on to Gordon's place for a sauna. But I haven't been back to my cabin. Now, on this glorious late summer afternoon, I continue walking straight ahead.

When I come to the dip where the tamaracks grow, I stop
and call like a great horned owl, the way we always did. I walk
up the other side, where the masses of blueberries and cranberries
grow, toward the prize patch of *nagoon* berries, the most delicious
berries in the world—like tiny tart strawberries.

I reach the turnoff to my cabin. Although the ground here is a
little higher, the tall spruce alongside the trail is leaning. From
a distance, the cabin looks the same. But when I arrive I see that
it, too, is leaning—sinking back into the bog. The windows are
cracked and boarded up from the inside. The doorframe has
shifted so much that I would have to kick the door in to open it.

I decide not to go inside. I tell myself that it may not be
safe. But the truth is, I want to leave that space as it was, and
as it always will be in my memory. Standing here now, I feel no
sadness, only tenderness, and an unexpected sense of comfort
that this small mark of mine on the earth will soon disappear. I
remember a passage from John Haines:

> I may not always be here in these woods. The trails I
> have made will last a long time; this cabin will stand
> twenty years at least before it falls. I can imagine a
> greater silence, a deeper shadow where I am standing,
> but what I have loved will always be here.

I walk on beyond the cabin, down to the lake and out onto
the point where I used to go to listen. The ducks dabbling among
the cattails are the same—shovelers and lesser scaup. The shore-
line appears unchanged. And the little copse of clean white paper
birches across the way is as elegant as ever.

I lean back against the diminutive twin spruce trees where
John and I sat side by side for our portrait, filled with excitement
about the work ahead of us. Here in these woods, we dreamed

of changing the world. Now the world is changing in ways we couldn't have imagined, and the woods are sinking back into the earth. John and Gordon are gone. Other friends and neighbors have moved on or passed away. Alaska has changed. I have changed. Our dreams have failed. Yet I cannot let them go.

When I was sixteen, I heard a recording of E. E. Cummings delivering his *Six Nonlectures*, and I was struck by the way the poet intoned, almost *sang* this recurring refrain:

"*I am an artist. I am a man. I am a failure.*"

That last word startled and perplexed me. Although it somehow resonated with my rebellious adolescent sensibility, I was too young and too full of myself to understand what it might actually mean. But as I've gotten older, I've become more acutely aware of my own failings.

When Thoreau died, Emerson wrote an essay for *The Atlantic*. Remembering his younger friend, Emerson observed that he acted "as if he did not feel himself except in opposition."

As a young man I was reflexive in my rebellion. I had staked out the high lonely turf, and I was determined to defend it at all costs. In Thoreau, I saw a model of rebellion. Over time, I've also discovered a model of redemption.

Like all of us, Thoreau was a flawed human being. Contrarian by nature, he is sometimes criticized as profoundly misanthropic. But the life and work of that misanthrope inspired Gandhi, King, and many others. And in Thoreau I've come to see how one flawed person actually *can* change the world.

"*I am an artist. I am a man. I am a failure.*"

In some way, we are all failures. Yet, for me, the object of art and life is not success. It seems to me that the best any of us can do is try to conduct our lives so that, on balance, we give more than we take—from the earth, and from our fellow human beings.

Although I follow no established religion, I have faith. My faith is rooted in the earth. The practice of my art is the practice of my faith. And, as Cummings concluded:

"An artist, a man, a failure, must proceed."

Art is my own best chance for redemption. I intend to follow it as faithfully as I can until I draw my last breath.

Benediction

It's a late afternoon in early summer. The air is hot and still. I'm walking slowly through the bosque, winding my way among the mesquite and paloverde.

I've been down the arroyo, looking for birds at a spot where there's a waterhole for much of the year. I found neither birds nor water. On the way back now, as I so often do, I'm thinking about Alaska, remembering.

Up ahead I see a familiar cholla cactus, and I know I'm approaching the place where my wife and I have passed so many idyllic days together. I've been gone awhile. To let her know that I'm almost back, I stop, cup my hands around my mouth, and hoot like a great horned owl.

She doesn't answer, but I'm not surprised. She knows that when I do this, I'm invoking Gordon. And here I am—eleven years after that night we carried his body down the mountain, and thousands of miles to the south—still calling the way he and I always called back and forth to each other in the taiga.

I lower my hands and continue walking. Suddenly, in an explosion of wings, a great horned owl swoops up in front of me!

At the last instant, the owl veers off and lands on the top of a tall cardón cactus, forty paces away.

I fall to my knees in the sand. As my tears flow, I speak to the owl, quietly voicing my gratitude for all that we shared in those days—the music, the friendship, and the dreams that still sustain me.

Swallows circle above, hunting in the deepening glow. The owl and I sit silently watching each other, for I don't know how long.

Eventually, I speak to him again: "I'm still here. I'm doing the best I can, following the music, trying to keep the vision alive."

As if in acknowledgment, the owl rises and floats off down the arroyo.

The bell tones of the canyon wren come showering down from the cliffs above.

ACKNOWLEDGMENTS

On a winter evening walk across frozen Lake Louise in the Alaska Range, the writer and critic Alex Ross asked me whether I'd ever considered writing a memoir. I hadn't.

"You've lived an interesting life," Alex said quietly.

I was flattered. Yet I couldn't help but wonder if his observation might suggest a corollary to the apocryphal Chinese curse: "May you live in interesting times." Perhaps an equally invidious wish might be: "May you live an interesting life."

Clearly, we are living in the most "interesting" of times. And whether or not my own life may be interesting in any other sense, I'm fairly confident that mine has not been the typical life of a composer. Even so, I'd always figured that memoirs were written by movie stars or politicians, or by people of truly extraordinary accomplishment. Since I don't fit any of those descriptions, writing a memoir didn't seem like something I would do. Even so, Alex's inquiry stuck with me and, almost a dozen years later, the result is this book.

Yet Alex Ross's most decisive contribution to this book was introducing me to his friend the editor Alex Star. For whatever reason, Alex Star took the leap of faith that there might be a book hidden somewhere in the first unruly manuscript he read. Several drafts later, we arrived at something that both he and I felt worthy of publication. Every exchange with Alex has been a pleasure, and our journey together has been a great learning for me.

I also want to acknowledge Ben Ratliff, who, in a chance encounter at baggage claim in LaGuardia Airport, encouraged me to send my manuscript to his publisher, Farrar, Straus and Giroux.

It would be understandable if a writer of the stature of Barry Lopez were to be mild about the literary aspirations of his composer friend. Instead, Barry has consistently and enthusiastically encouraged me to believe that I have stories to tell and the words to tell them. Barry's luminous writing and his faithful friendship have nourished me for decades.

The stories in this book are not only mine. For more than forty years now, my beloved wife, Cynthia, has been my partner in everything. Cynthia and I have shared countless amusements and adventures, joys and disappointments, losses and discoveries. Cynthia patiently read every iteration of this book, reminding me of details I'd forgotten while keeping me focused on the big picture, contributing her typically wise and witty insights. These are her stories as much as my own.

I want to thank Michael Agger at *The New Yorker*, Bryan Lowder and Forrest Wickman at *Slate*, and Ron Spatz at *Alaska Quarterly Review* for publishing earlier versions of parts of this book, and Peter Matson and Jane Rosenman for reading my initial rough drafts.

I'm grateful to Philip Glass for his singular music, and for the quiet support and generosity he has extended to me, as he has to so many others; to Tim O'Donnell for his brilliant legal mind, and his rapier wit; and to Molly Sheridan for keeping me pointed in the right direction, and for her assiduous attention to detail.

There are hundreds of other friends, colleagues, and collaborators whose faith, foil, inspiration, provocation, encouragement, and contention have shaped my life and work. I cannot name them all. But I am grateful to each and every one.

SOURCES

My life and my work have been shaped by many books and writers; notable among these are:

Henry David Thoreau
Walden

John Haines
The Owl in the Mask of the Dreamer
The Stars, the Snow, the Fire

Barry Lopez
Horizon
Arctic Dreams

Annie Dillard
Pilgrim at Tinker Creek

Edward Abbey
Desert Solitaire

Paul Shepard
Thinking Animals
Nature and Madness

Richard K. Nelson
Make Prayers to the Raven

Henry Cowell
New Musical Resources

John Cage
Silence

Lou Harrison
Music Primer

Throughout my life as a composer, I've found inspiration in the music of the birds, from the wood thrush (*Hylocichla mustelina*) and hermit thrush (*Catharus guttatus*), to the canyon wren (*Catherpes mexicanus*).

I've learned much from the gagaku music of Japan, the gamelan music of Java and Bali, Tibetan Buddhist ceremonial music, drumming and chant traditions of Africa, and especially the music of my Athabascan, Yup'ik, and Iñupiat friends and neighbors in Alaska.

Again and again I've returned to European music, from Johannes Ockeghem and Claudio Monteverdi to Johann Sebastian Bach, from Claude Debussy and Jean Sibelius to Iannis Xenakis and Eliane Radigue.

But my primary musical family is American, extending back several generations, including these and many other composers.

Charles Ives	Morton Feldman
Edgard Varèse	Pauline Oliveros
Henry Cowell	James Tenney
Ruth Crawford Seeger	Alvin Lucier
Dane Rudhyar	Robert Ashley
Harry Partch	Lois V. Vierk
John Cage	Peter Garland
Lou Harrison	Michael Byron
Conlon Nancarrow	Kyle Gann

Readers who are interested in hearing my music may find these recordings useful points of departure:

songbirdsongs
(Mode Records)

In the White Silence
(New World Records)

The Light That Fills the World
(Cold Blue Music)

Strange and Sacred Noise
(Mode Records)

Inuksuit
(Cantaloupe Music)

The Wind in High Places
(Cold Blue Music)

Become Ocean
(Cantaloupe Music)

Canticles of the Holy Wind
(Cantaloupe Music)

Become Desert
(Cantaloupe Music)

Those who want to read more about the music may find these books and this film of interest:

Winter Music: Composing the North
John Luther Adams
(Wesleyan University Press)

*The Place Where You Go to Listen:
In Search of an Ecology of Music*
John Luther Adams
(Wesleyan University Press)

*The Farthest Place: The Music of
John Luther Adams*
Bernd Herzogenrath, editor
(University Press of New England)

Strange and Sacred Noise
A film by Leonard Kamerling

A NOTE ABOUT THE AUTHOR

John Luther Adams was born in Meridian, Mississippi, and attended the California Institute of the Arts before moving to Alaska in 1978, where he lived until 2014. He was awarded the Pulitzer Prize for Music and a Grammy Award for his orchestral composition *Become Ocean*, which was premiered by the Seattle Symphony Orchestra in 2013. He is also the author of *Winter Music: Composing the North* and *The Place Where You Go to Listen: In Search of an Ecology of Music*. Since leaving Alaska, Adams has lived in New York City and in the deserts of Mexico, Chile, and the southwestern United States.